THE LIFE OF
LEONARDO
DA VINCI

THE LIFE OF LEONARDO DA VINCI

BY GIORGIO VASARI

·

EDITED BY MARTIN KEMP

·

TRANSLATED BY MARTIN KEMP
AND LUCY RUSSELL

40 ILLUSTRATIONS

Frontispiece: *The Last Supper*, 1495–98, detail.
Oil and tempera on plaster, 4.6 × 8.8 m
(181⅛ × 346½ in.).

The Life of Leonardo da Vinci
© 2019 Thames & Hudson Ltd, London

Text © 2019 Martin Kemp
Translation © 2019 Martin Kemp and Lucy Russell

Designed by Lisa Ifsits

First published in 2019 in the United States of America
by Thames & Hudson Inc., 500 Fifth Avenue,
New York, New York 10110

www.thamesandhudsonusa.com

Library of Congress Control Number 2018945044

ISBN 978-0-500-23985-8

Printed in China by RR Donnelley

CONTENTS

PREFACE AND
ACKNOWLEDGMENTS

Roger Thorp of Thames & Hudson asked if I thought it would be a good idea to produce an illustrated English edition of Giorgio Vasari's *Life of Leonardo*, drawn from the massive *Lives of the Most Excellent Italian Architects, Painters and Sculptors from Cimabue until our Time*, the founding work of art history, first published in 1550 and then in a heavily revised edition in 1568. I answered yes, enthusiastically, and confirmed that Vasari's account was a prime source of reference for anyone interested in Leonardo's art. I come to the edition as someone who has written extensively about Leonardo, and have set it up from this perspective.

A new edition seemed like a good opportunity to re-examine one of the most compelling of Vasari's *Lives*, to accompany it with a suite of high-quality illustrations, and to integrate the original and expanded texts in a way that would allow the reader to see what belongs in which edition. In 1909 Herbert Horne (founder of the Horne Museum in Florence) published an admirable though somewhat outdated translation of the 1568 edition, with informative annotations, but there has never been an English translation of those passages in the first edition that did not feature in the later one.

First thanks go of course to Roger, who has been the chief facilitator throughout. The designer, Lisa Ifsits, devised the ingenious typographical means for differentiating what appeared in the two editions, and dealt with the design problem of Vasari's relatively short text and a largish cluster of illustrations. Jen Moore worked with skill and care to make the text work to its best effect.

In the production of the integrated text of the two editions, Lucy Russell of Oxford University has played a key role. She studiously identified the differences between the 1550 and 1568 texts, translated the sections unique to the first edition and devised our first integrated text in both Italian and English, using colours and fonts to identify which was which. I have benefited from our discussions of crucial elements in the translation. Vasari was writing at a time when the vocabulary for writing about the visual arts was in the process of formation and not wholly stabilized. What now seems the obvious translation might not best convey what Vasari was trying to say. This translation aims to convey the 16th-century flavour of Vasari's vocabulary and syntax while making his texts accessible to a modern reader. He was for the most part having to invent a way of writing about artists and their productions with very limited precedents.

That my books offer repeated thanks to Caroline Dawnay of United Agents, with her able assistant Sophie Scard, and to my own personal assistant, Judd Flogdell, does not mean that the thanks have become routine. Their support has been unstinting. It was Caroline who introduced me to Thames & Hudson, who earlier published my *Living with Leonardo: Fifty Years of Sanity and Insanity in the Word of Art and Beyond*. Judd valiantly brings order to the incipient chaos of my life, particularly necessary with the 500th anniversary of Leonardo's death looming this year. A circle of personal friends acts as 'test readers' to see if what I am saying makes sense outside a specialist context. Trinity College Oxford, which I am delighted to serve as an honorary fellow, continues to provide a warm welcome, not least when I meet visitors, and I am grateful to the History Faculty for housing my library of Leonardo books.

There has been a tendency among some recent historians to debunk Vasari in general and the *Life of Leonardo* in particular. Working on the present edition has made me respect him more rather than less. He continues to provide a hugely engaging introduction to this most extraordinary of artists.

GIORGIO VASARI PIT. ET
ARCHITET: ARETINO

I

Title-page of *The Life of Giorgio Vasari*, 1568.

INTRODUCTION:
VASARI'S *LIVES* AND
THE *LIFE OF LEONARDO*

No account of the history of any cultural activity is more seminal than Giorgio Vasari's *Lives of the Artists* – or, to give it its full title, *The Lives of the Most Excellent Italian Architects, Painters and Sculptors from Cimabue until our Time, Described in the Tuscan Language, by Giorgio Vasari Aretine Painter. With a Useful and Necessary Introduction to their Arts.*[1] It was first published in 1550, in two very substantial volumes containing more than 280,000 words. A revised and substantially enlarged edition, almost three times as long, was published in 1568 in three volumes. Such a vast literary output was a monumental achievement for someone who was a very prolific painter and architect, and not a writer by education or profession. By 1568, 175 artists were honoured with their own biographies within the work, to say nothing of those who appeared under collective titles or received other mentions. Among this anthology, there is no more striking and entertaining *Life* than that of Leonardo.

At the heart of Vasari's vision was a great narrative of progress in the arts of architecture, painting and sculpture, beginning with

[FIG. 1]

the first tentative enlightenment around 1300, after the dark bar-
barities of the Gothic age. Next came gradual developments in
the emulation of classical antiquity and the imitation of nature,
before the third and culminating period of 'perfection' in which
the true ideals of the arts were fully realized, above all in the
person of Michelangelo. Leonardo was the founding artist of the
latter period. To read Vasari's successive *Lives* is to visit a great
museum of the mind, as if we are in effect walking through a
massive version of the Uffizi Gallery in Florence with a garrulous
guide, who is bursting with information, trenchant opinions,
picturesque stories and instructive messages. In fact, to walk
through the successive rooms in today's Uffizi is to follow a path
first laid out by the author of the *Lives*, both conceptually and lit-
erally. The literal dimension comes from the fact that Vasari was
[FIG. 2]   the architect of the 'offices' (*uffizi*) for his patron, Duke Cosimo
I, from 1560 onwards. What we now know as a series of galleries
of varied size and grandeur was actually planned to house the
Medici regime and its legislators. It was only after Vasari's death
that the bureaucrats and lawyers were displaced by works of art,
arranged in keeping with Vasari's majestic progression, though
modern visitors assume that this Vasarian parade of art was the
original function of the building.

    Many of the world's major galleries follow the chronological
and geographical progression of styles and functions first clearly
outlined in the *Lives*. The very idea of the *progression* of culture
– though not invented as such by Vasari – remains obstinately
dominant in the way we present the visual arts, and even other
cultural manifestations, including science and technology.

2
The Uffizi, with the Palazzo Vecchio
in the background.

All this is from the son of a potter (a *vasaio*, or 'maker of vases') from Arezzo, the Tuscan provincial city whose chief claim to artistic fame is the cycle of frescoes of the *Miracle of the True Cross* by Piero della Francesca in the Basilica of San Francesco. In his autobiography, Vasari constructed an inflated artistic lineage for his ancestors. He was indeed related by marriage to Luca Signorelli, but the painter from Cortona died when the author was just twelve years old. His first proper apprenticeship was to Guillaume de Marcillat, a French painter and maker of stained-glass windows who was working in the Cathedral in Arezzo. Crucially for his young charge, Guillaume knew about Rome's artistic scene from his period of employment at the Vatican. Such was Giorgio's promise that the Cardinal of Cortona took him to Florence and effected his first introduction to the Medici, whose patronage was to dominate the major phase of the artist's career. After some kind of brief attachment to Michelangelo, his most sustained training was with Andrea del Sarto, whose gracious style was deeply imbued with Leonardesque features.

Vasari's early career as an independent artist saw him travelling extensively in Tuscany and Umbria, and to major Italian cities, including Venice, Bologna, Naples and Rome. He later testified that he was scrutinizing works by local masters and had begun to accumulate notes on what he saw. It was in 1546, at a dinner in Rome hosted by Pope Paul III – according to Vasari's embroidered account – that the project of the *Lives* was hatched. The prime catalyst seems to have been Paolo Giovio, physician, senior cleric, historian and biographer, who had published *Eulogies of Illustrious Men of Letters* (or *Learned Men*), which included compact appreciations of Dante, Petrarch and Boccaccio. Giovio also wrote unpublished accounts of Leonardo, Michelangelo and Raphael.[2] He characterized Perugino as the eclipsed predecessor of the High Renaissance masters, just as Vasari was to do in his first edition of the *Lives*. In Giovio's perceptive and accurate account, Leonardo emerges as an exceptionally learned artist, much involved with anatomy and other sciences, capable of extraordinary things but prone to leaving works unfinished. It was Giovio who recorded that the French king (named as Louis XII) wanted to transport the *Last Supper* across the Alps. He also created an extensive museum of portraits of famous people, providing a precedent for the framed images of the artists that precede each of the biographies in Vasari's second edition of the *Lives*. Both men were convinced that character could be read reliably from faces. More generally, Giovio provided Giorgio with regular encouragement. When Vasari's book was being prepared for its first printing in 1547, it was sent to Giovio for approval, which it rapturously received: 'this will make you certainly immortal'.³

While assembling the *Lives*, Vasari had been gaining a reputation as a painter of rhetorical altarpieces and densely populated narratives that openly demonstrated his knowing mastery of the modern manner of painting. This involved a figure style informed by that developed by Michelangelo, homage to ancient sculpture, rhetorical gestures, meaningful faces and skill in overcoming the 'difficulties' of art (most notably elaborate poses and foreshortening). His is a consciously 'arty' art, in which the content tends to become a vehicle for style. His paintings now seem admirable rather than lovable. When the *Lives* were conceived, he was providing intricately designed narrative frescoes in Rome's Palazzo della Cancelleria, portraying the life of Pope Paul III in illusionistic settings. An inscription provided by Giovio boasts that the whole ensemble was improbably completed in '100 days'.⁴

Vasari's high productivity and political amenability made him the perfect artist for Cosimo I de' Medici, Grand Duke of Florence, and the publication of the *Lives*, with its dedication to

the Cosimo, played a significant role in his becoming favoured
as the dominant painter and architect at the court. Vasari was
the obvious choice when the Duke wanted someone to master-
mind the conversion of the grand interiors of the republican
Palazzo della Signoria (Palazzo Vecchio) into a visual assertion
of Medici magnificence, past and present. Vasari as architect
and painter was employed to refashion the palace of the former
government as the grandest of ducal residences. The central suite
of public frescoes Vasari was to paint, a visual cacophony of
military conquests, was in the massive hall of the great council, which had been built by the republican regime and which
housed Leonardo's unfinished *Battle of Anghiari*. The hall, now
[FIG. 3]   the 'Salone dei Cinquecento', was extensively remodelled and
extended in height. Leonardo's masterpiece was to disappear
(seemingly forever) under the wide swathe of Vasari's murals.

Medicean cultural patronage was lauded alongside their military and political prowess. Employment of major architects,
sculptors and painters had become a matter of prestige and
a demonstration of Tuscan leadership in art as in war. Cosimo
I was portrayed by Vasari in a ceiling roundel in the 'Sala di
[FIG. 4]   Cosimo' magisterially surrounded by the architects and engineers
who were transforming the fabric of the city into a civic theatre
for Medici rule. The two most prominent acolytes are Battista
del Tasso on the left, holding his model for the New Market, and
Niccolò Tribolo, displaying schemes for two of the fountains for
which he was famed. At the base of the roundel, Vasari himself
brandishes an architectural plan and twists to look knowingly at
the spectator. The participants are dressed in a strange mixture

3
A modern fashion show in Vasari's 'Salone dei Cinquecento',
Florence, Palazzo Vecchio.

4
Giorgio Vasari, *Cosimo I de' Medici with his Architects and Sculptors*,
roundel in the vault of the 'Sala di Cosimo' in the Palazzo Vecchio.

of contemporary and *all' antica* clothing, signalling the fusion of the ancient past with the glorious present.

Cosimo's approval of the statutes of the Accademia delle Arti del Disegno in 1563 was part of a consistent strategy to exploit the arts as a sign of Florentine cultural supremacy. The brainchild of Vasari, the Academy was the first to be founded anywhere, and provided the model for many later art academies across Europe. It had been preceded in 1540 by the Accademia Fiorentina (or Accademia degli Umidi) devoted to literary matters, not least to the promotion of Tuscan as the supreme Italian language. Vasari was careful to note that his *Lives* were 'described in the Tuscan language', overtly alluding to this Florentine claim.

As the master of all things visual at the Medici court, Vasari pursued a hugely successful career in Florence, and more broadly in Tuscany, with periods in Rome and elsewhere. He also took advantage of his ability to travel extensively in Italy, scouring cities in his long quest to gather material for his huge publication. In the last year of his life he embarked on the prestigious frescoes of the *Last Judgment* inside Brunelleschi's great dome of Florence Cathedral, but he died in 1574 before the project was finished. He was buried in Arezzo in an ample family chapel that he had designed, and which originally housed his very grand altarpiece of the *Miraculous Draught of Fishes*.

Vasari could look back on his own life with justifiable pride. He would certainly have wished (and might have expected) to be regarded as one of the greatest artists of his time. He is now considered an 'important' painter and architect, but not in the league of the elite succession of 'genius' painters about whom he had written, from Giotto to Michelangelo. Most visitors to Florence do not go specifically to see Vasari. But Giovio was right when he prophesied that the *Lives* would bring Vasari immortality.

GIORGIO'S FLORENTINE BOOK

Looking at Vasari's own life, the obvious question is, how did he manage to fit in so many projects, some on a very large scale? Three of the answers must be very hard work, remarkable efficiency and a great deal of energy. The fourth, and not the least, must be teamwork. As an architect commissioned to create large buildings, like the Uffizi, he would necessarily have acted as a contractor and employer, even if the payments were made from the ducal treasury. To cover the acreage of walls in the Palazzo Vecchio, not least in the Salone dei Cinquecento, he needed not just pupils but senior assistants who could reliably produce work invulnerable to charges that it was below the required standard. This collaborative model becomes relevant when we think about how he could have written his *Lives*. At one time it was tacitly assumed that the volumes were entirely written by Vasari, as the author's name on the title-page declared, though it was of course recognized that he must have made use of a large network of informants in a variety of geographical centres in order to cover all the mainstreams and tributaries of Renaissance art so comprehensively. More recently, it has been proposed that Vasari incorporated extensive passages drafted by associates, most of whom possessed literary skills beyond Vasari's. One scholar has suggested that only 40 per cent of the *Life of Leonardo* in the 1550 edition was composed by Vasari himself.[5] Although we would expect collaborators to be duly acknowledged in modern works, this was not the case in the 16th century. Vasari's senior assistants in the Salone dei Cinquecento, who were of a status to practise as independent painters in their own right, are all embraced under the collective name of Vasari as the author of the murals.

The *Lives* are very variable in how they are cast, ranging from accounts that proceed steadily through the artist's life and productions to vividly coloured literary portraits of individuals whose careers act as exemplars (sometimes cautionary) in matters artistic, personal and ethical. There are reasons why this should be, in addition to collaboration. Vasari accumulated material over an extended period, writing up the *Lives*, together with the opening sections on the arts of architecture, sculpture and painting, and the prefaces to the three parts, in between his many other jobs. A clear sign of the protracted authorship and editing process is that the preface to Part I does not mention the tripartite scheme of progress, which is instead introduced in the preface to Part II. In the 1568 edition, this second part culminates with Luca Signorelli, Vasari's esteemed relative, at the end of whose life he signals the arrival of Part III, whereas in the first edition, the final artist in Part II is Raphael's master, Pietro Perugino, without any obvious reference to the imminent arrival of the supreme masters of Part III. The tripartite scheme was not there from the first but evolved and was refined over time.

Sometimes even Vasari's extensive travels left him with scant material about a particular master. Artists from more distant eras were harder to characterize than those for whom local memories were still alive. He must have tapped into such local knowledge, soliciting accounts from his wide range of contacts in cities with which he was less familiar or never even visited. The uneven flavour of the *Lives* speaks to some kind of collaboration – just as we can sometimes distinguish different 'hands' in a work of art. For example, the preface to the first part, with its learned and detailed account of the history of art from Babylonia to the Middle Ages, displays levels of research and arcane knowledge likely to have been beyond Vasari himself. It is probable that learned colleagues at the Florentine court furnished written accounts that Vasari could incorporate.[6] Some *Lives* of recent or contemporary artists may have been assigned substantially to those who had all the necessary information to hand. The conjoined *Lives* of the architects Giuliano and Antonio da Sangallo are cases in point. However, looking at the *Lives* as a whole, the tenor of the great majority of the text seems to me to be distinctively Vasarian, and he should be regarded as their 'author'. Certain of the key words that deal with special qualities applied to art and artists are judiciously and consistently deployed across the *Lives*, implying a sole author (though perhaps future statistical analysis will shed further light on this question).[7] One of the key terms used by Vasari to designate an exceptional talent far beyond the norm is *ingegno*.[8] This does not quite carry the modern sense of 'genius', but it does designate an inborn excellence that cannot be acquired by effort. The frequency with which it appears in the *Lives* of those major artists endowed with *ingegno* is carefully judged. Before the Renaissance it was almost unknown for artists (as craftspeople) to be credited with *ingegno*. It became a signal term in the growing literature on the visual arts. Giotto warrants the epithet on three occasions, very respectable for an artist practising in the very first period of enlightenment, while in the next century Lorenzo Ghiberti registers a creditable five, Donatello a surprisingly meagre three, and Brunelleschi a remarkable seventeen. The architect of the Florentine dome had been prominently credited with *divino ingegno* in the memorial tablet mounted on the wall of the Cathedral beneath his sculpted bust in 1446, and was clearly regarded as an exceptional citizen in all respects. Leonardo merits twelve *ingegni*, Raphael six and Michelangelo twenty-two (in a *Life* four-and-a-half times as long as Leonardo's). The innate quality of *ingegno* was closely related to *virtù*, which indicated outstanding worth and merit, associated integrally with character, ethics and morals. It is here that the pious, principled and unyielding Michelangelo excels, being accorded *virtù* an astonishing sixty-three times in contrast to Leonardo's five. The implication is that had Leonardo's *ingegno* been more closely allied with *virtù*, he might have been less capricious in his approach to his primary profession of painting. That being said, Leonardo's transcendent talents were recognized as *divino* on fourteen occasions, standing proudly alongside those of the 'divine Michelangelo' (as that painter was known in his own lifetime).

Such a carefully judged deployment of key terms indicates that a single mind was in charge of the overall system of evaluation in the *Lives*, particularly the major ones. It may well be that the *Lives* of lesser artists, more obscure by dint of reputation and/

or geography, relied particularly heavily on material submitted by other authorities. And we have already noticed that the learned preface to Part I lay substantially outside Vasari's scope.

In addition to drawing on the knowledge of his far-flung contacts, Vasari used any earlier accounts of art and artists on which he could lay his hands. He certainly knew Lorenzo Ghiberti's *Commentaries*, a copy of which was owned by Cosimo Bartoli at Cosimo I's court.[9] This was particularly valuable for information regarding painters of the first enlightenment period. Antonio Manetti's *Life of Brunelleschi* provided vital substance for Vasari's laudatory account of the great architect.[10] Francesco Albertini's pioneering guide to the 'many statues and pictures' in the city of Florence was very useful.[11] There were also small unpublished assemblages of artist's lives and works upon which Vasari could draw,[12] along with the long verbal tradition of stories in the artist's studios, which featured the kind of pithy and moralizing wit in which Florentines excel. Like all stories, they no doubt became enhanced in the telling. Vasari must have been a relentless pesterer of anyone he thought could give him snippets of information.

We know that Vasari did not lack support from highly sophisticated literary men in Florence. The very authorities who wrote about literature, constructing the cultural myths of Tuscany in the Florence of Cosimo, were those who were supporting Vasari's building of the arts of *disegno* into the picture. *Disegno* in this sense means not just draftsmanship but the highest manual dexterity in the expression of natural and cerebral beauties. The most important of Vasari's literary friends was Vincenzo

Borghini, a learned Benedictine cleric who had fingers in many cultural pies in Medicean Florence and had built up a discerning private collection of Italian art.[13] Borghini was deeply involved in the founding of the Accademia del Disegno and with the lavish commemorations for the death of Michelangelo in 1564, though it was Vasari who directed the work on the elaborate sculpted and painted wall-tomb to the 'divine' master in Santa Croce, the principal Franciscan church in Florence. Borghini was Vasari's 'iconographer', devising the topics for his friend's narratives and allegories in the Palazzo Vecchio. He was particularly influential in determining how the greatly expanded edition in 1568 should work. He encouraged a more overtly 'historical' approach that granted greater attention to solid documentation, and pressed Vasari to increase his geographical coverage, to which Vasari responded by visiting no fewer than thirty-five different cities in four months in 1566, ranging from Papal Rome to Venice and Milan.

Borghini instructed his friend to concentrate on the artistic achievements of his subjects, rather than dwelling on the particulars of *Lives* that in themselves could not match those of the 'great men' of history:

> The goal of your work is not to write the lives of painters, nor to say whose sons they were or what ordinary deeds they accomplished, but only their WORKS as painters, sculptors and architects;....Writing lives is solely for princes and men who have accomplished princely things, and not for lowly people.[14]

The new emphasis was to shift the narrative from a succession of individuals to a sense that their works were cumulatively contributing to the achievement of the final goal of art.[15]

Not least, Borghini undertook the considerable task of providing what Vasari calls 'copious' indexes for the second edition of the *Lives*. There was a dense index devoted to names, a selection of 'notable things' (such as envy between practitioners) and a very extensive list of locations, compiled with great care. For example, under 'Florence, San Salvi', Borghini noted 'a picture. Verrocchio, [p.] 465'; and later 'an angel in the said picture. Lionardo da Vinci, [p.] 565'. We may well imagine that Borghini's close reading extended into editorial work, and he sent Vasari a plentiful supply of motivational letters.

We can see how Vasari's *Lives* were shaped to fit with the enterprise of the literary academicians with whom he associated. Cosimo Bartoli, who was prominent as an adviser to Vasari, included musicians and artists within his book on the Tuscan language. He also wrote about techniques of terrestrial measurement, which Vasari utilized in the landscapes that provide the settings for his battles and sieges. Bartoli published editions of writings by Leon Battista Alberti, whose book *On Painting* from 1435/6 was the pioneering treatise on the theory of art. It seems highly likely that material was provided for the first and perhaps also later prefaces by Bartoli and Pierfrancesco Giambullari, a linguist and historian of ancient Tuscany, who acted as editorial intermediary between Vasari and the publisher.[16]

There were other learned colleagues with whom Vasari interacted. Perhaps the most notable was Benedetto Varchi, once exiled from Florence because of his republican sympathies, but brought back by Cosimo I. Varchi, a keen advocate of the Tuscan vernacular, was commissioned to compile a substantial account of Florentine history, which he undertook between 1527 and 1538. In 1547 he delivered a lecture to the Florentine Academy in which he provided a philosophical commentary on Michelangelo's sonnet, 'The excellent artist has no concept [that one single block of marble does not enclose]'. This was published in 1549 with a second 'lesson' devoted to an elaborate *Paragone* (comparison of the arts of sculpture and painting), in which he published letters he had solicited from Vasari, Bronzino, Pontormo, Tasso, San Gallo, Tribolo, Cellini and Michelangelo (who was very rude about Leonardo's denigration of sculpture).[17] It is clear that the visual arts were now an integral part of Florentine high culture.

The printers were very much part of the same Florentine cultural industry. The publisher of the first two-volume edition of Vasari's *Lives* in 1550 was Lorenzo Torrentino, a Dutch typographer, printer and humanist scholar imported by Cosimo to advance the city's publishing industry to top international standards. Torrentino's books, with handsome and ingenious frontispieces by Florentine artists, have a look of their own. After the printer's death in 1563, the second edition was published by the distinguished house of Giunti in Florence in 1568. As the title-page declares, these volumes of the *Lives*, now three in number, were 'newly revised with their [the artists'] portraits, and with the addition of new lives of the living and of the dead from 1550 to 1567...with tables [indices] in each volume of the most notable things, the lives of the practitioners, and the locations where their works are'.[18] Leonardo's *Life* was one of those subject to substantial amplification.

THE *LIVES* OF LEONARDO

In both editions Leonardo's *Life* opens Part III, devoted to those fully enlightened artists who moved decisively beyond the limitations of the second period into the third and final period, which Vasari called the 'modern'. We have noted that the painter who closes Part II in the first edition was Pietro Perugino, while this role is reassigned in the revised edition to Vasari's relative Luca Signorelli, who 'by the fundamentals of design and especially of nudes, and by his grace of invention and the composition of his scenes...opened the way for the final perfection of art'. But no one in the second period could take this vital step. As Vasari explains in his preface to the culminating section of the *Lives*,

> Leonardo...initiated the third style or period....In
> addition to the vigour and bravura of his draftsmanship
> and his most subtle reproduction of all the details
> of nature precisely as they are, according to good rule,
> superior order, correct proportion, perfect design
> and divine grace, most abundantly copious and most
> profoundly skilful, he truly granted to figures motion
> and breath.

Vasari, viewing things as always through Tuscan spectacles, goes on to state that Giorgione, when he initiated the modern age in Venice, was following Leonardo.

The *Life of Leonardo* follows a familiar, if not invariable, pattern for the more substantial *Lives*. The typical biography opens with a lively assessment of the individual's qualities as an artist and his essential character – two things that were as one in Vasari's system of values.[19] He considered that each artist's works were an expression of his inner being (indeed of his 'soul'), and that his physical characteristics were similarly determined, including his physiognomy, actions and general behaviour. The portraits in the 1568 edition were important expressions of this conviction – not only the artists' physiognomies but also what can be seen of their costume and headwear.[20] Altogether there were 144 portraits within their decorative frames, while 8 frames remained empty, because no portrait was available.

The unflattering profile portrait of Leonardo in the illus-
[FIG. 5]   trated edition does not correspond closely to what had become the artist's accepted likeness in the 1 century, and is notably different from the authentic profile portrait in a red chalk drawing
[FIG. 6]   by an unknown artist, which is often attributed to Francesco Melzi. Vasari may have based his likeness of Leonardo on an image in Giovio's collection. Also in this second edition Vasari lists the remarkably extensive collection of portraits of famous men from all spheres of religious, political, military and cultural activity that were housed 'in the museum of the most illustrious and excellent Signor Cosimo'. These were displayed in the aerial corridor that Vasari built across the river from the Palazzo

LIONARDO DA VINCI PITT.
E SCVLTOR FIOR.

5

Portrait of Leonardo da Vinci
in the 1568 edition of Vasari's *Lives*.

6
Portrait of Leonardo by an unknown associate, *c.* 1500.
Red chalk, 27.5 × 19 cm (10⅞ × 7½ in.).

Vecchio to the Palazzo Pitti via the Ponte Vecchio in 1564. The idea was that how somebody looks is vital in understanding how they act.

Not infrequently, Vasari's written portraits of the artists carried an exemplary message for those wishing to practise the arts – and, by implication, any other profession. Paolo Uccello, for example, early in the second period, 'would have been the most delightful and capricious *ingegno* since Giotto' if he had not become wholly obsessed with the geometry of perspective, neglecting figures and perpetrating a 'dry style'. He was endowed by nature with a disposition that was 'solitary, eccentric, melancholy and poor'. Uccello's *ingegno* was real but thus warped. Verrocchio, Leonardo's master, is praised for his versatility in various media, but his style of painting was 'hard and crude, lacking any sweetness', being the result of indefatigable effort rather than natural gifts. Verrocchio's effort and constrained measure of *ingegno* justified his place among 'rare and excellent artists', but he is nowhere credited with the highest of innate talents that would lift him to the very top rank.

The introduction to Leonardo's *Life* emphasizes that his gifts were not natural, but supernatural: they were the gift of god. The artist's mental endowments were complemented by grace of appearance and remarkable strength, as was required in Vasari's system of body and soul. In his first edition, Vasari included a spectacularly effusive passage to indicate the 'divine nature' of Leonardo, who does not just 'represent humanity but the divine itself'. This was omitted in the second edition. Vasari might have been embarrassed by the hyperbole, but it is more likely that he

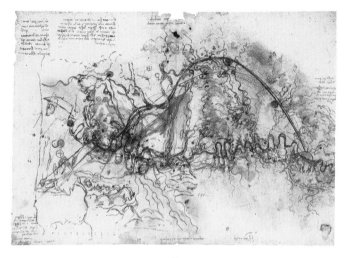

7
Scheme for the Arno Canal, c. 1503. Brush and ink over black chalk,
pricked, 33.5 × 48.2 cm (13¼ × 19 in.).

wished to reserve the highest levels of divinity for his personal
artistic god, Michelangelo Buonarroti.

What then typically follows in the larger *Lives* is some account
of the child who begets the man. Vasari liked stories of the artist's
early training, in which his essential nature is already discernible
in nuce. In both the first and second editions Vasari tells us that
the boy Leonardo was very brilliant, confounding his teachers,
but was already showing signs of the variousness that diverted
him from one thing to another. However, since Leonardo was
always drawn back to the arts of design, his father, Ser Piero da
Vinci (in 1550 Vasari thought him the boy's uncle, but corrects

this in 1568) showed Leonardo's drawings to Verrocchio. There is in fact a documented link between the lawyer and the sculptor. In 1470, acting in his legal capacity, Ser Piero recorded that Verrocchio had rented out a house with a shop and a well to a certain Giovanni di Saccardo.[21] The property was on the corner of the Via dell'Agnolo and Via dei Macci, near the Via Ghibellina and close to Ser Piero's office. The shop is currently occupied by a frame-maker.

Verrocchio studied the drawings and was 'stupefied' to see how far innate talent had taken the young man, before he had had any formal training. Taken into the sculptor's workshop at some point in the later 1460s, the young Leonardo demonstrated his versatility in the arts of design, a versatility that is described more expansively in the second edition. Here as elsewhere, Vasari is able to adduce actual drawings that he himself had collected and mounted in his Libro de' Disegni, each drawing supplied with an elegant frame drawn in pen, ink and wash.[22] In this early stage of the *Life*, Vasari makes reference to the many kinds of things Leonardo did later in his career, not least in engineering, including the Arno canal, with which Leonardo was involved [FIG. 7] around 1503. The gossipy story of Leonardo's plan to raise the Florentine Baptistery on a pedestal of steps, which features in both editions, would also belong much later in his career.

Along with these additions to the early part of the revised *Life*, there was an important excision. Vasari removed entirely a sentence about Leonardo as a 'heretic' who was more drawn to philosophy than religion. It is probable that Vasari had formed this view upon seeing what is now called the Codex Leicester in

8
Andrea del Verrocchio and studio, *Baptism of Christ*, c. 1474–76.
Oil and tempera on panel, 177 × 151 cm (69⅝ × 59½ in.).

the hands of Giuseppe Porta, the sculptor, architect and engineer, in Rome. The outer folios of Leonardo's notebook deal with the nature of the moon, which is described as a planet much like the earth. They also deal with vast changes in the 'body of the earth' over huge tracts of time. Leonardo daringly rejects the Biblical deluge as the cause of the presence of fossils in high mountain strata. Why did Vasari drop the sentence? It has been suggested that the Counter-Reformation, a campaign to reassert the worldwide rule of the Catholic Church, was impinging on his willingness to cite Leonardo as a heretic. But the excision is more likely to have been the result of Vasari's meeting with Francesco Melzi, the Milanese nobleman who was the keeper of Leonardo's drawn and written legacy. Melzi's intervention is, as we will see, very evident in a number of places in the *Life*, including the fuller account of Leonardo's diverse activities that we have already noted. Melzi clearly showed Leonardo's manuscripts to Vasari.

There follows a series of examples of the young Leonardo achieving extraordinary things. His angel in Verrocchio's *Baptism of Christ* so far surpassed his master's figures that Andrea vowed   [FIG. 8] never to touch colours again. Leonardo's intervention, which modern scientific analysis has shown to extend beyond the angel, was already noted in Albertini's early artistic guidebook to the city. The young painter's cartoon for the tapestry *Adam and Eve in Paradise* is praised as a miracle of naturalism. The cartoon, apparently unfinished, was seen by Vasari, but seems now to have vanished without trace. Leonardo also manipulates nature in the terrifying and stinking monster that he assembles from components of repulsive animals, the image of which he paints on a peasant's shield that his father had asked him to decorate. What has happened to the ugly buckler that terrified Ser Piero? Vasari prefaces his account with 'it is said', leaving the reader scope to doubt its veracity. Throughout the *Lives*, Vasari told stories that were true in spirit if not in pedantic fact, like the writers of *novelle*, the genre of short stories at which Italian authors excelled. The same may be true of the painting of the *Head of Medusa*, which does not feature in the 1550 edition, but Vasari again testifies that he has actually seen it. The account of the horrible Medusa, with his coiffure of writhing snakes, also gives Vasari the opportunity to describe Leonardo's characteristic drawings of bizarre faces and extravagant hair.

The problem that Vasari faced while recording Leonardo's early career is that he knew very little about those few works that we now assign to the period before his departure to Milan in 1481/2. Vasari did not know about the *Annunciation*, the *Benois Madonna* or (in the first edition) the unfinished *Adoration of the Magi*. It does seem, however, that the *Madonna* owned by Pope Clement VII is that now in Munich. He did know about the *Portrait of Ginevra de' Benci* but placed it after 1500. In the second edition he does mention the unfinished *Adoration*, which had such an effect on Raphael and other painters, but only passingly.

His account of Leonardo's departure for Milan as a kind of artistic emissary from Lorenzo de' Medici, taken from the Anonimo Gaddiano (an anonymous text once owned by the Gaddi family), is credible if not demonstrable. Leonardo was known for his abilities on the *lira da braccio*, an ancestor of the

[FIG. 24]
[FIG. 36]
[FIG. 28]

[FIG. 9]

9

Marcantonio Raimondi, *Orpheus Charming the Animals (Leonardo with a Lira da Braccio?)*, *c.* 1508. Engraving, 21.4 × 17.3 cm (8⅜ × 6¾ in.).

10
Study for Judas, c. 1495.
Red chalk on red prepared paper, 18 × 15 cm (7⅛ × 5⅞ in.).

viola, and was interested in the design of novel instruments of the kind that Vasari describes.[23] It seems that the musician, Atalante Migliorotti, was sent to Milan at the same time, and remained at the court, as did Leonardo. In 1568 Vasari dates Leonardo's arrival in Milan to 1594, when Ludovico formally became Duke of Milan, but this is twelve years too late.

Vasari knows a good deal about Leonardo's two greatest artistic projects in Milan, the *Last Supper* and the bronze equestrian memorial to Ludovico's father, Francesco. The great narrative mural was certainly known to artists in Florence and Rome, including Raphael and Andrea del Sarto (Vasari's master), via descriptions, copies and drawings. Vasari may not have seen the actual painting before 1550, but he was aware that it centred on the compelling reactions of the disciples to Christ's announcement of Judas's impending betrayal. Vasari recounts the painting's striking naturalism, and in a short and eloquent sentence, he singles out the tablecloth as a passage of supreme verisimilitude, which indeed it is. He introduces a recurrent motif in the *Life* to explain why Christ's head remained unfinished, namely that the painter was habitually striving for an ultimate truth that could never be realized by human hands. The apparent lack of finish was, in reality, the result of the early deterioration of the mural's painted surface.

[FIG. 30]

[FIG. 10]

In the second edition, Vasari introduces a substantial and entertaining anecdote about the importunate Prior of Santa Maria delle Grazie, where the *Last Supper* was making characteristically slow progress. The story had earlier been retailed by Giambattista Giraldi, a north Italian poet and man of letters.[24]

Vasari again prefaces his version with 'it is said that...', giving us reason to question its veracity. Irritated by Leonardo's protracted and contemplative manner of working – or not working – the Prior complained to the Duke, who felt that he had no choice but to call Leonardo to account. When they met, the painter gave Ludovico an impromptu lecture on the nature of 'elevated *ingegni*', who often did major work (of a cerebral kind) when they appeared to be doing nothing. He also explained, much to the Duke's amusement, that he was vainly seeking a model for the malign features of Judas, but would use those of the Prior if no other image came to hand. Leonardo also tells his patron of his unavailing search for a face that could match that of the 'incarnate divinity' of Christ.

Even after seeing the *Last Supper* on his rapid tour in 1556, Vasari did not feel it necessary to make changes to his earlier description of the great mural, even though he included in his second account other things he had learnt on his visit to Lombardy. He did insert a reference to the damaged mural in the *Life of Garofalo and Girolamo da Carpi, Ferrarese painters; and other Lombards*, which was added to the second edition. He records that Fra Girolamo Monsignori in San Benedetto in Mantua 'portrayed the most beautiful Last Supper in Milan by Leonardo da Vinci, copied so well that I was amazed. I am pleased to have this new record of it, having seen the original in Milan in 1566, which has come down to us so poorly that nothing more is apparent than a glaring stain. Thus the piety of the good father perpetually renders homage in this place to the great merit [*virtù*] of Leonardo.' Fra Girolamo's less than astounding copy, reduced in height to just above the disciple's heads, is now in the Museo Civico A. E. Baruffaldi in Badia Polesine.

The fame of Leonardo's project for the truly massive horse of bronze – its ducal rider is rarely mentioned – spread far and wide. An extensive series of studies survive, but the project's ulti- [FIGS 34, 35] mate failure became a source of ridicule for him. Vasari reports the opinions of those who concluded that Leonardo deliberately began 'impossible' projects in the grip of some kind of delusion of grandeur. Vasari counters, quoting the poet Petrarch, to the effect that 'the work was held back by desire'. Leonardo's fault was that of striving for 'excellence beyond excellence and per-fection beyond perfection'. If a flaw could be admirable, this one was. In any event, the huge clay model that Leonardo had created was destroyed by the invading French in 1499, as Vasari explains in his *Life of Giuliano da Sangallo*, and Leonardo's ability to realize it in bronze was untested.

Noting in the second edition that Leonardo researched the anatomy of horses for the model, as he indeed did, Vasari inserts a long and laudatory account of the master's researches into human anatomy. He was particularly impressed by the wonder- [FIGS 11, 12] ful studies of the bones and muscles from around 1510, which may well have been undertaken with the surgeon Marcantonio della Torre in Pavia, as Vasari says. He regretted that the accom-panying texts were written back-to-front in 'ugly' characters by Leonardo's left hand. One needed a mirror to read them. The source for this enhanced awareness of Leonardo as an anatomist is openly acknowledged as 'Messer Francesco Melzi, Milanese gentleman, who in Leonardo's time was a very beautiful young

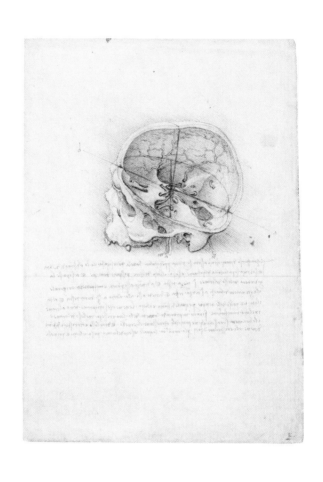

11
Sectioned Skull, 1489.
Pen and ink, 19 × 13.7 cm (7½ × 5⅜ in.).

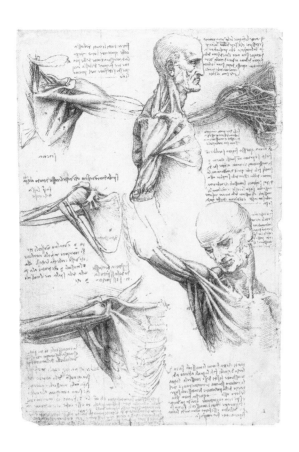

12
Anatomy of the Shoulder, Breast and Neck, with a
Wire Diagram of the Muscles, c. 1510. Pen and ink with
wash over black chalk, 29.2 × 19.8 cm (11½ × 7¾ in.).

man, much loved by him, just as today he is a beautiful and kind old man who guards the pages with care, like relics'. There can be no doubt that Melzi knew the *Life* in the first edition, and was keen to set the record straight in some key respects. Given this account of Leonardo's anatomies, the brief mention of them in the later section on the *Battle of Anghiari* was taken out of the 1568 edition.

Vasari had also come to learn of what seems to be one version of the *Treatise on Painting*, then in the hands of an unnamed Milanese painter who was seeking without success to have it printed. This may have been Gian Paolo Lomazzo, a prominent painter and a major theorist in Milan, for whom Leonardo was a key point of reference.[25] An abridged version of Leonardo's *Treatise on Painting* did indeed become known in intellectual circles in Cosimo's Florence, but seemingly too late to exercise an influence on the 1568 *Life*.

Vasari (like us) is better informed about Leonardo's second main period in Florence than his first. He rightly singles out Leonardo's project for one or more paintings of St Anne, a popular republican saint in Florence. There seem to have been at least three cartoons containing various permutations of the Virgin, Child, St Anne, the infant St John the Baptist and the sacrificial [FIG. 13] lamb. Only one survives. The cartoon Vasari describes as exhibited to much acclaim in Santissima Annunziata for two days – an incredibly innovative thing to do – was similar but not identical [FIG. 14] to the painting in the Louvre. Vasari gives a notably perceptive account of the cartoon, and records in the second edition that it went to France. Vasari had reason to be well informed about

13
Cartoon for the Virgin, Child, St Anne and St John, c. 1507–8.
Charcoal (and wash?) heightened with white chalk on paper,
mounted on canvas, 141.5 × 104.6 cm (55¾ × 41⅛ in.).

14
Virgin, Child, St Anne and a Lamb, c. 1507–16.
Oil on panel, 168 × 130 cm (66⅛ × 51⅛ in.).

Santissima Annunziata. He was an apprentice in the workshop of Andrea del Sarto, who had worked for the monks of the Annunziata for fifteen years, living next to the convent as their trusted artist.

The Annunziata is also a locus for Leonardo's knowledge of Francesco del Giocondo, Mona Lisa's financially astute husband. In 1526 the fathers of the Annunziata granted Francesco permission to construct his family tomb in the Chapel of the Martyrs, prominently located in the great centralized choir.[26] The focal point of the choir was the large high altar, for which Leonardo had once been expected to provide paintings, as Vasari records. The period of Vasari's apprenticeship coincided with the decoration of Francesco's Chapel. There was no shortage of people to whom Vasari could have turned for information about the portrait of Lisa. Francesco's son, Piero, lived close to Giorgio [FIG. 37] from 1555, and could have intervened if he felt that the 1550 account was defective. When Vasari says that Leonardo worked on the portrait for four years before leaving it unfinished, this is consistent with the known starting date of 1503 and Leonardo's departure from Florence in 1507. It is very unlikely that Vasari saw the portrait, but not wholly impossible. It is first recorded in the king's collection in France in 1550 by Vasari himself. What is important and remarkable is that Vasari devoted one of his most striking pieces of word painting to a portrait of a bourgeoise Florentine woman who was of no significance outside her immediate circle. Vasari, like those who directly encountered the *Mona Lisa*, knew that it was sensational as a *picture*. He knew enough about the portrait to know that he had to pull out all the stops in his toccata of praise for one of the greatest masterpieces of all time. The vivid account that he first set down in 1550 remained untouched in 1568.

[FIGS 15, 16] Vasari was even closer to Leonardo's other major Florentine project, the mural of the *Battle of Anghiari*, since what remained of it occupied one of the walls in the large republican council hall that Giorgio himself aggrandized in the mid 1560s as the reception hall within the palace that the Medici were taking over. He knew that Leonardo was allocated the large Sala del Papa in the monastery of Santa Maria Novella to produce the massive cartoon from many sheets of paper pasted on a supportive backing. His account of the ingenious scaffolding invented by Leonardo so that it could be lowered and raised at will is consistent with the payments Leonardo received, and his description of Leonardo's ill-fated attempt to paint on the wall as if it were a panel primed for oil painting also matches the documentation and other accounts. Vasari's pacey description of Leonardo's central knot of savagely fighting soldiers and equally savage horses may depend on what survived of the cartoon, as well as what remained of the unfinished painting and various copies. The *Battle* exhibited everything that Vasari admired: supreme *disegno*, swathes of anatomical knowledge, complexity of motion, daring foreshortening, effortlessly inventive details, compositional skill and compellingly dramatic storytelling. This being said, it is surprising that he does not recognize Niccolò Piccinino, 'Milanese captain', as the gap-toothed warrior screaming at the top of his voice at the centre of the melee. He does not mention the Florentine warriors by name, no doubt conscious that

15
Peter Paul Rubens, *Copy of Leonardo's Battle of Anghiari, c.* 1603 (original
c. 1503–6). Black chalk, pen in brown ink, brush in brown and grey ink,
grey wash, heightened in white and grey-blue, 45.3 × 63.6 cm (17⅞ × 25 in.).

16
Copy of the Battle of Anghiari, also known as the 'Tavola Doria', 1503–5.
Oil on panel, 86 × 115 cm (33⅞ × 45¼ in.).

his Medicean paymasters were not inclined to praise republican heroes. Equally, there is no reason to think that Vasari had much of a conscience while covering the wall surfaces in his rebuilt hall with his own complex depictions of Medicean campaigns of military action. If he did find a way of conserving Leonardo's unfinished mural under his new walls, which is very unlikely, the chance of anything surviving 500 years later is slim.

Leonardo's second period in Milan between 1507 and 1513, punctuated by travels, disappears in Vasari's *Life*. There are no major artworks that are omitted as a consequence. Wearing his Medicean hat, Vasari picks up the story when Leonardo travels with his patron, Giuliano de' Medici, on the election of Giovanni de' Medici as Pope Leo X in 1513. In the extended papal court, Leonardo reverts to his earlier role as a biological trickster. He invented hollow animals that could be inflated like balloons and released to fly tempestuously in the air for a brief time. He transformed a strange lizard into a kind of living dragon. And he scraped fat from the guts of a bullock so that the thin but elastic tissue could be inflated to fill a fair-sized room. We can easily write these off as Vasari's fantasies. However, there were memories of Pope Leo's Roman era in Vasari's Florence thirty years later, and we know that Leonardo could exercise his sense of humour to entertain idle courtiers. Vasari is aware that Leonardo was involved with mirrors for Giuliano, looking to construct huge concave mirrors that could generate the kind of heat that Archimedes was supposed to have utilized to burn enemy ships. He also squeezes in two actual works of art in the second edition, a *Madonna* now unknown (if indeed it was a work by Leonardo) and a portrait of a young boy, perhaps the cheery *Boy with a Puzzle*, now attributed to Bernardino Luini, in the Proby Collection at Elton Hall near Peterborough.

In a short account of Leonardo's final years in France, Vasari rightly mentions the painting of *St Anne* made from one of the cartoons, but seems uncertain if it was finished. Otherwise, the French years are dominated by the intense piety Leonardo expressed as he neared his meeting with his Creator. Vasari's stress on Leonardo's Christian beliefs is reworded in the second edition to imply that the master painter did not so much 'return' to the true faith as strongly affirmed it, regretting that he had not respected his own talents as a painter. Leonardo's death itself, romantically narrated as occurring in the loving arms of the French king, served Vasari's campaign to elevate the status [FIG. 39] of artists. We have first-hand testimony that Francis I indeed regarded Leonardo with the greatest favour. Benvenuto Cellini, whom Vasari knew well, largely as an antagonist in Cosimo's court, reported that:

> King Francis, being enamoured to the very highest degree of Leonardo's supreme qualities took such pleasure in hearing him discourse that he would only on a few days in the year deprive himself of Leonardo....I cannot omit repeating the words I heard the King say about him.... He said that he did not believe that a man had ever been born in the world who knew as much as Leonardo, not only of sculpture, painting and architecture, but also that he was a very great philosopher.[27]

17
Giovan Francesco Rustici with Leonardo,
Preaching of St John the Baptist, c. 1506–11. Bronze.

Leonardo's *Life* is rounded out with a summary of, and ful-
some praise for, his qualities. In terms of his art, Vasari singles
out Leonardo's 'shadowed manner' as giving a special power to
modern painting. He adduces the three bronze figures in Rustici's
[FIG. 17]   *Preaching of St John the Baptist* as evidence of how Leonardo's
disegno can be expressed in sculpture. The anatomies of horses
and men again receive special mention. Finally, his 'divine' attributes are stressed, before a eulogistic epitaph that features in both
editions, transcribed in capital letters, proclaims that Leonardo
had routed the Greek masters, Phidias and Apelles.[28] At the
very end, brief and downbeat references are made to the least

unworthy of Leonardo's pupils, Giovanni Antonio Boltraffio and
Marco d'Oggiono, which have not been included in the present
translation.

In his role as pioneer of the third great art style of the
Renaissance, Leonardo is praised elsewhere in the *Lives* as a significant influence on Piero di Cosimo, Fra Bartolommeo and
Lorenzo di Credi (a fellow alumnus of Verrocchio's workshop).
The most substantial reference occurs in the *Life of Raphael*, in
the course of a section added to the 1568 edition to explain the
trajectory of Raphael's' artistic career:

> When he [Raphael] saw the works of Leonardo da Vinci,
> who had no equal in the qualities that he gave to heads
> of men as well as women, and who in giving grace to his
> figures and their motions surpassed all the other painters,
> Raphael was left wholly stupefied and amazed. In short,
> the style of Leonardo pleased him more than any other he
> had ever seen, and he set himself to studying it, leaving
> behind little by little the style of Pietro [Perugino], if only
> with great effort. He sought, to the extent of his knowledge
> and ability, to imitate the style of Leonardo. But for all his
> diligence and the studies he made, he was never able to
> surpass Leonardo in some of the challenges of art. And if it
> may well seem to many that he had surpassed Leonardo in
> his sweetness and in a certain natural facility, nevertheless
> he was never superior to Leonardo's special fundamental
> intensity of concept[29] and the grandeur of his art, in which
> few bear comparison to Leonardo. But Raphael came

closer to Leonardo than any other painter, above all in the graciousness of his colours.

This paean of praise in the *Life of Raphael* serves as a very effective summary of Leonardo's merits, at least as much as anything in the *Life of Leonardo* itself.

It is easy to point out what Vasari got wrong in his *Life of Leonardo*, and what he missed; in total he discusses only eight paintings, overlooking ten or so. But he does identify the artistic landmarks in Leonardo's career, each of which are celebrated in compelling descriptions. Above all, he paints a fascinating picture of an artist and polymath of true genius, who fought perpetually to realize ideas that ultimately lay beyond even his divine reach. No *Life* in Vasari's three mighty volumes is more vivid than that of Leonardo.

NOTE TO THIS EDITION
AND TRANSLATION

Earlier editions and translations

Since Vasari's expanded three volumes of the *Lives* were published in 1568, well over a hundred editions have been released in a number of languages. Patricia Lee Rubin's *Giorgio Vasari: Art and History* provides a good overview of the editions and the translations. The first comprehensive critical edition in Italian was by Gaetano Milanesi, who in nine volumes (1846–1855) annotated Vasari's text with copious references to a wide range of documentation and known works of the artists. Among subsequent Italian editions, the most useful is that by R. Bettarini and P. Barocchi (1996–99), which includes both the 1550 and 1568 editions of Vasari's original work.

The first translation of the *Life of Leonardo* into English was in William Aglionby's *Painting Illustrated in Three Diallogues, Containing some Choice Observations upon the Art. Together with the Lives of the Most Eminent Painters* (London, 1685). Leonardo's *Life* was one that he chose to translate in a lively and perceptive manner. The first full set of English *Lives* was published in five volumes in 1852 by the shadowy Mrs Jonathan [Eliza] Foster. Her rather free style of translation has been criticized, but she conveys the tone of Vasari's texts in a readable manner. This was followed by Allen B. Hinds in 1900, whose translation gained wide diffusion in Dent's Everyman's Library. In 1943 Ludwig Goldscheider included Hinds' translation, adding his own annotations in his useful assemblage of sources in his Phaidon monograph, *Leonardo da Vinci*. Gaston du C. de Vere's well-regarded, mainly literal translation of the complete text in ten volumes appeared between 1911 and 1914 and is still available in the Everyman's Library series, effectively introduced by David Ekserdjian. The free translations in George Bull's selections from the *Lives* for Penguin Classics (1987) have not been generally admired by scholars, but have provided a fluent introduction to Vasari for general readers. The more recent and careful translations of selected and edited *Lives* by Julia and Peter Bondanella in 1991 has remained in print with Oxford World Classics.

The only book specifically devoted to a translation of Vasari's *Life of Leonardo* was published in 1903 by Herbert Horne, founder of the evocative Museo Horne in Florence and author of an excellent monograph on Botticelli. Horne's edition can still be consulted with profit for his scholarly annotations to Vasari's text. He also included what were then serviceable illustrations of works mentioned by Vasari.

The present translation

The aim of this new translation is to remain faithful to Vasari's original while making his text accessible to a modern reader. This involves a tricky balance, since Vasari's style of writing is generally typical of the period and specifically reflects his own ways of thinking. The passages at the beginning and end of the *Life* present the greatest problems. When eulogizing Leonardo's unique characteristics, Vasari is drawn into a rhetorical mode that can become very convoluted. These passages have been adapted to a greater extent than his accounts of particular incidents and individual works of art. The main structural intervention has been to break up some of Vasari's extended sentences, and to divide his lengthy paragraphs, both of which are hard work for those accustomed to current prose styles. Vasari's vocabulary and syntax has generally been maintained in the translation, unless his meaning became obscure in modern English.

We have been alert to where the modern meanings of some of the words used by Vasari differ from his intent, particularly with regard to the loaded terms prevalent in the writing about art at this time. In the introductory essay I have discussed *ingegno*, which is not quite the same as modern 'genius'. We have translated it in ways that seemed appropriate in each context, occasionally as 'genius' when this read best. *Virtù* (worth, merit, virtue) is a comparably key term, full of meaning in the Renaissance. Again, it has been translated according to context. *Disegno* is an even more momentous term. It means 'drawing' or 'draftsmanship' in its modern translation, but Italian Renaissance usage is more ambitious, carrying implications of high graphic skills placed in the service of the visual concepts in the artist's mind. It applies across all the arts, fine and applied. The Accademia del Disegno was dedicated to providing a wide visual education for artists that included matters of anatomy, perspective and light and shade. Vasari refers to those who practise the visual arts as *artefici*. This has often been translated as 'craftsmen', but this would be right for *artigiani* ('artisans'). Vasari's *artefici* is related to the Latin word *artifex*, which means 'artificer' or 'maker', both of which would sit rather oddly in the text. Here we use the more neutral (if not wholly satisfactory) 'practitioners'. It is worth noting that *sfumato*, a term now commonly used to describe Leonardo's manner of painting and meaning 'softly blended', or 'like smoke', does not occur in Vasari's *Life of Leonardo*, and hardly elsewhere in the *Lives*. In fact, it was a term rarely used by Leonardo himself, and certainly not one he privileged.

This is the first edition in any language that has blended the 1550 and 1568 texts. Wherever Vasari made a substantial change, either by the omission of passages from the earlier edition or by substantial amplifications in the later edition, these are signalled by specific colours. In a few places the flow of the text may be slowed somewhat by flagging the additions and excisions, but the gains seem to outweigh the minor losses. Less substantial changes that do not significantly affect the sense are signalled in the footnotes, to avoid interrupting the fluency of the revised narrative. The brief addendum at the end of the *Life* mentioning two of Leonardo's pupils (Giovanni Antonio Boltraffio and Marco d'Oggiono) has not been included.

The illustrations in the translated text are of paintings or projects known to Vasari, together with some drawings that he either knew of or which correspond to the kinds of things he is discussing.

Grey text indicates passages in the 1550 edition
that were omitted from the 1568 edition.
that were omitted from the 1568 edition.
Brown text indicates passages new to the 1568 edition.
Black text appeared in both editions.

THE LIFE OF LEONARDO DA VINCI, FLORENTINE PAINTER AND SCULPTOR

BY GIORGIO VASARI

The greatest gifts are often seen to rain down in a natural way on human bodies through celestial influences, and sometimes supernaturally, combining beauty, grace and merit fulsomely in a single body.[1] These gifts are made apparent whenever such a man turns his attention to something. His action is so divine that he leaves in his wake all other men, making it clearly evident that this quality arises (as it does) from the gift of God and is not cultivated by human artifice. Men saw this in Leonardo da Vinci, in whom there was not only beauty of body – never praised enough – but also a more than infinite grace in all his actions. Such was his resulting virtue that whenever his mind turned to difficult matters, he wholly resolved them with ease. The strength within him was conjoined with dexterity, and his soul and his courage were always regal and magnanimous. And the fame of his name grew so widely that it was not only held in esteem in his own time but also increased in posterity after his death.

Now and then the heavens truly send us those who do not represent humanity alone but the divine itself, so that from the divine in them, we can approach with our talent and the excellence of our intellect the highest spheres of the heavens, imitating the divinity of these exemplars as a model. From experience one sees those who, with some incidental study, turn to follow in the footsteps of these miraculous souls. If they are not helped by nature, since they are not the same as those souls, they at least approach the divine works that participate in their divinity.

Truly˙ miraculous and celestial was Leonardo, son° of Ser Piero da Vinci.⁺ In learning and in the foundations of literature˙ he would have made great profit if he had not been so various and unstable. For he set out to learn many things, and, having made a start, abandoned them. Thus, in the few months that he attended to the abacus, he made such strides that he was led to raise continual doubts and difficulties with the master who was teaching him, very often confounding his teacher.² Then he was given to working with music for a time, resolving to play the *lira* [*da braccio*], as one who by nature possessed an elevated spirit and was full of refinement; accordingly, he improvised song in a divine manner.³

Nevertheless, although he had attended to so many different things, he never gave up drawing and modelling in relief, as something that appealed to his imagination more than any other thing. Seeing this and considering the level of his talent, Ser Piero one day took some of his drawings to Andrea del Verrocchio, who was a good friend of his, and directly asked him if he could

˙ Thus
° nephew
⁺ who truly was a very good uncle and relative to him, helping him through his youth and especially
˙ in which

[FIG. 9]

say whether Leonardo would profit in some way from being set to the art of design. Andrea was astonished to see the very considerable start made by Leonardo, and assured Ser Piero that he should be assigned to such study. Accordingly Ser Piero arranged that Leonardo should enter the workshop of Andrea; Leonardo willingly followed this course. He did not follow just one line of work, but all those involving the art of design. And having an intellect so divine and miraculous, and being such a very good geometer, he not only worked in sculpture and in architecture, but he wanted his profession to be painting.

Nature showed in Leonardo's actions such high talent that in his ability to reason silenced scholars with explanations of a natural kind. He was alert and intelligent, and with perfect art of persuasion showed the complexities of his mind, making calculations of how to transport mountains, pull weights, and, among other things, making in his youth several heads of smiling women in terracotta, which are still cast in plaster, and similarly he made heads of infants, which appeared to have come from the hand of a master, but he also worked in architecture, making many drawings of plans and of various buildings. Although he was still young he engaged in discussions about the river Arno and the making of a canal between Pisa and Florence.[4] He made [FIG. 7] designs for flour mills and fulling mills and other devices that operate through the power of water.

Because his profession was to be painting, he studied in full measure how to draw from nature.[5] He often made models and [FIG. 18] figures in clay on which he placed rags infused with clay. Then he set out patiently to portray them on certain fine canvases of

18
Study of a Lily with the Plan of a Building, c. 1476.
Pen and ink and ochre wash with white heightening over
black chalk, outlines pricked, 31.4 × 17.7 cm (12⅜ × 7 in.).

19
*Study of the Drapery of a Kneeling Figure (perhaps for an Angel
in an Annunciation)*, *c.* 1476. Brush and tempera with
white heightening on paper, 18.1 × 23.4 cm (7⅛ × 9¼ in.).

[FIG. 19]
Rheims linen or on treated cloth, on which he worked with black
and white using the point of a brush. These were miraculous
works, as those that I have in our book of drawings still testify.
Furthermore he drew on paper with such care and refinement

[FIG. 20]
that no one has ever come close, and I have one of a head in stylus
and chiaroscuro that is divine. Granted to him by the grace of
God was such talent, and such an awesome display of intellect,
allied to the memory that served it, that with the art of design in
his hands he knew how to express his concepts most fully. In this
way he triumphed with his reasoning, and his logic confounded
every combative mind.

Every day he made models and designs so as to be able to
cut into mountains with ease and tunnel through them from
one level to another. Using levers, winches and jacks he showed
how to raise and drag heavy weights, and methods for dredging

[FIG. 21]
harbours and pumps to excavate low beds of water.[6] Thus his
brain never ceased devising things. His ideas and inventions are
to be seen in many surviving drawings within our profession, as I
have witnessed myself. In addition, he consumed time designing
knots of cord made following a system such that the cord can be
traced from one end to the other, arranged in such a way that it
fills a circular figure. This can be seen in a very demanding and

[FIG. 22]
beautiful print, in the middle of which are the words, 'Leonardus
Vinci Academia'.[7]

Among his models and designs, there was one, shown many
times to the ingenious citizens who then governed Florence, with
which he demonstrated his desire to raise the temple of San
Giovanni [the Baptistery] in Florence and insert steps below

20

Study of a Woman's Head, *c.* 1483. Silverpoint and white highlights
on prepared paper, 18.1 × 15.9 cm (7⅛ × 6¼ in.).

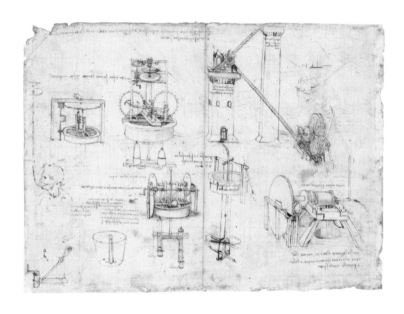

21
Design for Pumps, Archimedean Screws and Breathing Apparatus,
from *Codex Atlanticus*, fol. 1069r, *c.* 1478.

22

Knot Design, *c.* 1495. Engraving on laid paper after Leonardo, inscribed
'ACADEMIA LEONARDI VIN', 24.1 × 22.9 cm (9½ × 9 in.).

without ruining it. So powerful was his reasoning that he per-
suaded them it was possible, even though each person when they
had left him understood for themselves the impossibility of such
an undertaking. He was so pleasing in conversation that he drew
everyone's mind to his way of thinking.

Although we may say that he owned nothing and worked
but little, he always maintained servants, and horses that contin-
ually delighted him, and not least other kinds of animals, which
he looked after and cared for with great love and patience. This
was often demonstrated when passing through places where they
sell birds, taking them from their cages with his own hands,
paying the sellers the price they were asking, and releasing them
to fly in the air, restoring their lost liberty. Accordingly, nature
so favoured him that wherever he turned his thinking, his brain
and his soul, he exhibited such divinity in his acts that no one
has ever equalled him in perfection, vitality, goodness, elegance
and grace.

* One finds   It can readily be seen* that Leonardo, on account of his high
understanding of art, began many things and never finished
them. It seemed to him that his hand was not able to accomplish
in art the perfection of the things he imagined. Thus he conceived many complexities that were subtle and so marvellous that
with his own hands – even given their excellence – they could
never be realized. Such was his diversity that, philosophizing on
natural things, he strove to understand the properties of herbs,
and to persist in observing the motion of the heavens, the course
[FIG. 23]   of the moon and the passage of the sun. Thus he formed in his
mind a concept so heretic that he didn't approach any religion,

Light of the Sun on the Moon and Earth and the 'Ashen Light'
of the New Moon, from *Codex Leicester*, fol. 2r, c. 1508.

seemingly considering it far more important to be a philosopher than a Christian.

As we said earlier, he was assigned in his youth by Ser Piero, his uncle, to the study of art with Andrea del Verrocchio, who was making a picture in which St John was baptizing Christ, in which Leonardo worked on an angel who was holding some gar-
[FIG. 8]   ments.[8] Even though he was so young he accomplished it in such a manner that it was much better than the figures by Andrea that were located beside the angel of Leonardo. This was the reason why Andrea never again wanted to touch colours, dismayed that a young man understood painting better than he.

Leonardo was commissioned to provide a door hanging to be made in Flanders from woven gold and silk, for which he made a cartoon of Adam and Eve when they sinned in terrestrial Paradise.[9] With his brush, in chiaroscuro and with white heightening, he made a meadow with uncountable numbers of plants and many animals. It can truly be said that, in diligence and faithfulness to the natural world, no divine genius could have equalled it. There is a fig tree in which the foreshortening of the leaves and the appearance of its branches are carried out with such love that our understanding is dazzled just to think that any man could have such patience. There is also a palm tree in which the rotundity of the crown of the palm is constructed which such great artistry and illusion that anyone without the patience and mind of Leonardo could not have made it. However, the work was not taken further than this. The cartoon is today in Florence in the blessed house of the Magnificent Ottaviani de' Medici, to whom it was given not long ago by an uncle of Leonardo.

It is said that when Ser Piero, uncle of Leonardo, had gone to his villa, he was sought out by one of the country people who had made with his own hand a round shield [buckler] from a fig tree that he had cut down in his smallholding and which he wished to have painted in Florence. Ser Piero was very pleased and willing to do this since the peasant was very adept at capturing birds and in fishing, and was serving Ser Piero regularly in such matters. Thus Ser Piero took it to Florence without saying anything to Leonardo about whose it was, and he entreated him to paint something on it. One day, Leonardo took the buckler into his hands, and seeing that it was warped, badly worked and crude, he straightened it using fire and gave it to a wood-turner – rough and crude though it was – to render it smooth and even. After Leonardo had gessoed and prepared it in his manner, he began to think what might be painted on it and what would frighten anyone who came across it, producing the same effect that the head of Medusa had done. To this end, in a room where no one but himself was to enter, he took reptiles, lizards, crickets, snakes, butterflies, locusts, bats and other strange species of similar animals. From the multitude of these, variously assembled together, he contrived a gross animal, very horrible and frightening, with poisonous breath that enflamed the air. He showed this beast emerging from a dark and fractured rock, spewing poison from its open throat and smoke from its nose – so extravagantly that it seemed an absolutely monstrous and horrendous thing. In this room, where the animals had suffered the crudest of deaths, he did not himself smell the putrefaction, so concerned was he to make it and such was the great love he bore his art.

After this work was completed, neither the peasant nor
˙ uncle Leonardo's father˙ enquired after it. Leonardo then said to Ser
Piero that he could collect it at his convenience, since he considered it finished. Hence, one morning Ser Piero went to the room
for the buckler, and knocked at the door. Leonardo opened it
and asked him to wait for a moment. Returning to the room he
mounted the buckler in the light on an easel, and adjusted the
window so that the buckler was in dazzling light, and then he let
him see it. Ser Piero at first glance, not thinking about anything
in particular, was instantly shocked, not grasping that it could
be the buckler and not being aware that it was a painting that
depicted what he was seeing. As he turned to step away, Leonardo
restrained him, saying, 'this work has achieved what it was made
for. Take it and carry it away, because this is the end for which
the work was intended'. It seemed to Ser Piero that this was more
than miraculous, and he mightily praised Leonardo's capricious
conception. Next he quietly bought from a tradesman a buckler
painted with a heart pierced by an arrow. He gave this to the
peasant, who remained grateful for it as long as he lived. Next
Ser Piero secretly sold the one by Leonardo to certain merchants
for a hundred ducats. In short order it came into the hands of
Francesco the Duke of Milan,¹⁰ sold by the merchants for three
hundred ducats.¹¹

[FIG. 24]　　　Leonardo then made a picture of Our Lady, which was in
the possession of Pope Clement VII, which is very excellent.
Among other things that were in it, he reproduced a carafe full
of water containing some flowers. In addition to the marvellous
lifelikeness of the flowers, he had imitated the dew-drops of

24
Madonna and Child, c. 1475.
Oil on panel, 62 × 48.5 cm (24⅜ × 19⅛ in.).

25
Neptune and Sea Horses, c. 1505.
Black chalk, 25.1 × 39.2 cm (9⅞ × 15⅜ in.).

the water on them, so that they seemed more alive than life itself.

For Antonio Segni, his close friend, he made a Neptune on a sheet of paper, produced with draftsmanship of such diligence that it appeared wholly alive.[12] One could see the turbulent sea and the chariot pulled by marine horses, with fantastic creatures, sea monsters, personifications of the winds and other heads of marine animals, all most beautiful. This drawing was given by Fabio, Antonio's son, to Messer Giovanni Gaddi, with the following epigraph:

[FIG. 25]

Virgil depicted Neptune, as did Homer,
Steering his horses through the breakers of the resounding sea.
Their pictures are both observed within the mind,
Vinci's in our eyes; he is rightly victorious over both.[13]

The fancy came to him to paint a head of Medusa in oil on a panel, with a coiffure of knotted snakes – a stranger and more extravagant invention cannot be imagined. However, as happens with works that are time-consuming, and as happens with all his things, it remained unfinished.[14] This is among the excellent things in the palace of Duke Cosimo, together with the head of an angel who raises one arm in the air, which is foreshortened as coming forward from the shoulder to the elbow, and with the other arm he places his hand on his breast.[15]

It is a remarkable thing that this genius, having the ambition to endow the things he was painting with the strongest

modelling, went so far with dark shadows as to exploit the dark-
est grounds, seeking blacks to make deep shadows, darker than
the other blacks, and by their means to make his highlights seem
all the brighter. In the end this method of colouring was such
that no light remained there, and his pictures assumed the guise
of things represented at night-time, rather than in the brilliance
[FIG. 26]   of daylight. All this came from seeking to render things in greater
relief, and to achieve the ultimate perfection in this art.

It so pleased him when he saw some bizarre heads, or men
with beards or hair growing untamed, that he would follow one
that pleased him for a whole day, so fixing him in his mind as
an idea that when he arrived back in his house he could draw
it as if the man had been present. Of this type of drawing, it is
possible to see many heads of women and men, and I have several
drawn in pen by his hand in our book of drawings, which I have
mentioned before. One is of Amerigo Vespucci, which is a most
beautiful elderly head drawn in black chalk, and similarly that
of Scaramuccia, captain of the Gypsies, which was subsequently
owned by Messer Donato Valdanbrini of Arezzo, canon of San
[FIG. 27]   Lorenzo, left to him by Giambullari.[16]

[FIG. 28]   Leonardo began a picture of the Adoration of the Magi, in
which there are many beautiful things, especially the heads. This
was in the house of Amerigo Benci opposite the Loggia of the
Peruzzi, and remained incomplete like other of his things.

When Giovan Galeazzo, Duke of Milan, happened to
die, and Ludovico Sforza succeeded to that office in the year
1494, Leonardo, who had a huge reputation, was dispatched to
Francesco, the Duke in Milan.[17] The Duke greatly delighted in

26
St John the Baptist, c. 1508–15.
Oil on panel, 69 × 57 cm (27⅛ × 22½ in.).

27
Grotesque Head (Scaramuccia?), c. 1505.
Black chalk on paper, 38.2 × 27.5 cm (15 × 10⅞ in.).

28
Adoration of the Magi, c. 1480–81.
Oil on panel, 2.46 × 2.43 m (96⅞ × 95⅝ in.).

the sound of the *lira* [*da braccio*] when it was played.[18] Leonardo carried with him an instrument that had been made by his hand largely in silver, in the shape of a horse's cranium, which was extraordinary and new, in order that the harmony might be of greater fullness and more sonorous in tone, in this way surpassing all the other musicians who had come together to play there.[19] In addition to this he was the best reciter of improvised poems in his day. When the Duke listened to Leonardo's miraculous utterances, he became so enamoured of his talents that it was incredible to see. He begged Leonardo to make an altarpiece painted on a panel in which was a Nativity, which was sent by

[FIG. 29] the Duke to the Emperor [Maximillian].[20]

Then he made a Last Supper in Milan for the friars of San Domenico in Santa Maria delle Grazie, something that is very beautiful and marvellous, and the heads of the Apostles were endowed with much majesty and beauty, although that of Christ was left unfinished since he did not think it was possible to

[FIG. 30] convey the celestial divinity required for Christ. This work, left in this final state, is perpetually held in great veneration by the Milanese, and also by visitors from outside, in that Leonardo has imagined and managed to realize the suspicions that assailed the Apostles about who was to betray their master. To this end, their faces bear witness to love, fear and indignation, or rather sorrow, at not being able to embrace the thinking of Christ. This is no less a cause of wonder than our being confronted with the stubbornness, hate and treachery of Judas – without mentioning that every small detail of the work displays an incredible diligence. It thus happens that in the tablecloth he has replicated the work

29
Virgin of the Rocks, first version, *c.* 1483–94.
Oil on panel (transferred to canvas), 1.99 × 1.22 m (78⅜ × 48 in.).

30
The Last Supper, 1495–98.
Tempera on plaster, 4.6 × 8.8 m (181 × 346 in.).

of weaving in such a way that Rheims linen itself could not be closer to the truth.

It is said that the Prior of that place solicited him very importunately to finish the work, it seeming strange to him how Leonardo sometimes spent half the day immersed in thought. He would have preferred that Leonardo should never put his brush down, like a labourer who hoes soil in a garden. And if this was not enough, he complained to the Duke and stirred things up, so that the Duke was moved to send for Leonardo to expedite matters. He did this tactfully and in such a way as to indicate that all this was happening because of the importunity of the Prior. Leonardo, knowing the mind of the prince to be sharp and discerning, decided to talk at length with him about this matter (which he had never done with the Prior). He provided ample arguments about the nature of art and made him understand that when the greatest geniuses are working less they actually accomplish more. They are searching in their minds for inventions and shaping those perfect ideas that are then expressed and rendered by their hands – having already conceived them in their intellects. And he added that he still had two heads to complete, that of Christ, which he could neither find on earth or even envisage – as if he might presume that in his imagination he could conceive of that beauty and celestial grace demanded by divinity incarnate.

Leonardo was also lacking a head for Judas, which was occasioning him much thought, not thinking that it was possible to imagine a model who would serve as the face of someone so wicked that he would resolve to betray his Lord, the Creator of

the World, after receiving such favours. Even if Leonardo were
to continue seeking this second head, and in the end could not
find anything better, he would not be short of that of the Prior
– who had been so importunate and indiscreet. This statement
moved the Duke impulsively to laughter, and he agreed that
Leonardo had a thousand reasons on his side. So the poor confused Prior decided to press on with his work in his garden and
leave Leonardo alone. He fully finished the head of Judas, who
[FIG. 10]   served as the very image of treason and inhumanity. As was said,
that of Christ remained unfinished.[21]

The nobility of this picture, as much for its composition
as for its being finished with incomparable diligence, aroused
the desire of the King of France [Louis XII] to transfer it to
his kingdom. Hence he searched everywhere for architects who
could protect it with braces of wood and iron in such a way that
it could be transported securely, without regard to cost, which
he would indeed have done such was his desire. But since the
painting had been done on a wall, his Majesty could not realize
his intentions, and it remains for the Milanese to see.

At the top end of the same refectory there was a Passion in an
old style, and while Leonardo was working on the Last Supper,
he portrayed the aforesaid Ludovico with Massimiliano, his first-
born, and on the other side Duchess Beatrice with Francesco,
[FIGS   his other son, who later both became dukes of Milan, and who
31, 32, 33]   were divinely portrayed.[22]

While he was attending to this work, he proposed to the Duke
to make a horse of bronze of incredible dimensions, to create a
[FIGS 34, 35]   memorial to the image of the Duke.[23] He began and developed

it on such a scale that it could never be manufactured. There
are those who were of ˙ the opinion (as happens with human   ˙ There is
judgments that are often jealously malign) that Leonardo, as
with other of his works,° commenced it knowing that it could   ° the works he
not be finished. Being of such a size and intended to be cast in   produced
one piece, he started it in such a way that it was difficult to bring
to perfection; the sculpture could be seen to pose such incredible
difficulties that it is possible on this account to understand why
they made this adverse judgment, seeing that many of his works
did remain incomplete. But in truth we may believe that a mind
so very great and very excellent was encumbered by an excessive
will in aspiring to search for excellence beyond excellence and
perfection beyond perfection. It is for this reason 'that the work
was held back by desire', as our Petrarch has said.[24] And truly
those who have seen the large model that Leonardo made in
clay judged that they had never seen anything more beautiful or
superb. It survived until the French, who entered Milan under
King Louis of France, completely smashed it. Also lost is a little
model in wax, which was held to be perfect, together with a
book on the anatomy of horses made by Leonardo as part of
his research.

Leonardo next applied himself to the anatomy of men,
assisting and collaborating with Messer Marcantonio della   [FIGS 11, 12]
Torre, excellent philosopher, who was then lecturing in Pavia
and writing on anatomy, and was the first (as I have heard)
who began to illustrate the teachings of Galen on medical matters, bringing anatomy into the light, which until this time had
been enveloped by many great shadows of ignorance.[25] In this

31
Giovanni Donato da Montorfano,
Crucifixion, 1495 with later additions. Fresco.

32, 33
Portrait of Ludovico Sforza and his son Massimiliano (left) and
Portrait of Beatrice d'Este and her son Francesco Sforza (right), in Giovanni
Donato da Montorfano's *Crucifixion* (opposite), 1495 and 1497.

34
Proportions of a Horse owned by Galeazzo Sanseverino, *c.* 1493. Metalpoint,
pen and ink on prepared paper, sheet: 32.4 × 23.7 cm (12¾ × 9⅜ in.).

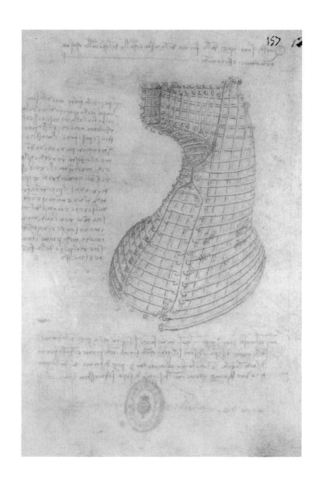

35
*Armature for the Piece-Moulds for the Casting of a Horse's
Head and Neck,* from *Codex Madrid, c.* 1498.

Marcantonio was marvellously served by the mind, labours and hand of Leonardo, who compiled a book drawn in red chalk and with texts written in pen in which he drew cadavers that he had dissected with his own hand and portrayed with the greatest diligence. He drew all the bony parts and joined all the nerves to these in due order, overlaying them with the first insertions of the muscles, and the second layer that holds the bones firm and the third that move them. On these pages, body part by body part, he wrote texts in ugly characters, made with the left hand in reverse, and those who are not familiar with them cannot understand them, because they cannot be read without a mirror. These pages on the anatomy of men are for the most part in the hands of Messer Francesco Melzi, Milanese gentleman, who in Leonardo's time was a very beautiful young man, much loved by him, just as today he is a beautiful and kind old man who guards the pages with care, like relics, together with a portrait of Leonardo of happy memory.[26] For someone who reads these writings, it seems impossible that this divine spirit could have understood so well the art of the muscles, nerves and vessels, and applied equal diligence to every part. There are also other writings by Leonardo in the hands of [...], a Milanese painter, similarly written in left-handed characters in reverse, which treat of painting and the methods of drawing and colouring.[27] Not long ago this man had come to Florence to see me, wishing to publish this work, and he took it to Rome to do this, but I do not know what then transpired.[28]

To return to the works of Leonardo, the King of France came at this time to Milan, and beseeched Leonardo to make

something extraordinary, and Leonardo made a lion that walked
several paces, and then opened its breast to reveal that it was full
of lilies.[29]

In Milan he took under his wing the Milanese Salaì, who
exhibited very delectable grace and beauty, having lovely hair,
abundant and curly, with which Leonardo was mightily pleased,
and he taught him many aspects of art.[30] Certain works that are
said in Milan to be by Salaì were retouched by Leonardo.

Returning to Florence he discovered that the Servite Friars
had commissioned from Filippino [Lippi] a work on panel for
the high altar of the Nunziata, about which Leonardo said he
would have willingly done something similar.[31] When Filippino
heard this, like the kind person he was, he stepped down. Because
Leonardo was to paint the altarpiece, the Servite Friars took him
into their house, providing expenses for him and his household.
He held this commission in abeyance for a long time, and never
commenced anything. Finally* he made a cartoon in which there   *In this
was Our Lady and St Anne, with a Christ Child, which not   manner
only amazed all the practitioners but when it was completed
was also placed in a room for two days where men and women,
old and young, came to experience the wonders of Leonardo, as   [FIG. 13]
if it were a solemn festival. It stupefied the whole population.
In the face of Our Lady, wholly simple and beauteous, could be
seen the simplicity and beauty with which the mother of Christ
is endowed. He wished to exhibit the modesty and humility of
a virgin most content and joyous to witness the beauty of her
son, supporting him tenderly on her lap. With a modest glance
downwards, she looks at a St John as a little boy who is playing

with a lamb, not without a smile from St Anne, full of joy at seeing her earthly progeny become divine.[32] Such were the true products of the intellect and genius of Leonardo. This cartoon, as indicated below, later went to France.

[FIG. 36]   He portrayed Ginevra, wife of Amerigo de' Benci, a very beautiful work, and he abandoned his work for the friars, who returned the commission to Filippino, who was then overtaken by death and was unable to complete it.[33] Leonardo undertook to make for Francesco del Giocondo the portrait of Mona Lisa, his wife, and after struggling with it for four years, he left it unfin-
[FIG. 37]   ished.[34] This work is now in the possession of the King Francis of France at Fontainebleau.

In this head, anyone who wishes to see how closely art could imitate nature may comprehend it with ease; for in it were counterfeited all those tiny things that only with subtlety can be painted, seeing that the eyes had that lustre and watery shine which are always seen in life, and around them were all the vivid rosy tints of the skin, as well as the eye lashes, which cannot be done without the greatest subtlety. The eyebrows, through his having shown the manner in which the hairs arise from the flesh, where more thick and where more sparse, and curved following the pores of the skin, could not be more natural. The nose, with its beautiful nostrils, rosy and tender, seemed to be alive. The mouth, with its cleft and its tips blending the red of the lips with the flesh-tints of the face, truly seemed to be not pigments but flesh. In the pit of the throat, if one gazed upon it intently, one could see the beating of the pulses, and in truth it may be said that it was painted in such a manner as to induce trembling and

36
Portrait of Ginevra de' Benci, c. 1478.
Oil on panel, 38.1 × 37 cm (15 × 14⅝ in.).

37
Mona Lisa, c. 1503–14.
Oil on panel, 77 × 53 cm (30⅜ × 20⅞ in.).

fear in every valiant practitioner of art, whoever he is. He also made use of this strategy: since Mona Lisa was very beautiful, while painting her portrait he always retained persons to play or sing and jesters, who continuously made her cheerful, in order to take away that melancholy that painters often tend to give to the portraits that they make. And in this work of Leonardo's there was a smile so pleasing that it was a thing more divine than human to witness; and it was held to be something marvellous, since it was not other than living.

On account of the excellence of the works of this divine practitioner, his fame grew to such an extent that all those persons who delight in art, and also the whole city, wished that he might leave behind him some monument to his talent. They debated how to get him to undertake some notable and grand work that would honour the public and honour the talent, grace and judgment with which they were acquainted in Leonardo's works. Together the Standard-Bearers and the leading citizens were engaged in newly constructing the great hall of the council, the architecture of which was taken in hand with the advice of Giuliano da Sangallo and Simone Pollaiuolo, known as Il Cronaca, Michelangelo Buonarroti and Baccio d'Agnolo (as is recounted in the corresponding sections of this book).[35] Having completed the hall with great haste, it was determined by public decree that Leonardo should be set* to paint some beautiful thing for it. Thus he received a commission for the hall from Piero Soderini, then the Standard-Bearer of Justice.

*and they wished him

Keen to comply, Leonardo began a cartoon in the Room of the Pope, located in Santa Maria Novella. The cartoon contained the story of Niccolò Piccinino, Milanese captain of Duke Filippo [Visconti], for which he designed a knot of horsemen contesting a standard, which is held to be most excellent and of great mastery for its marvellous treatment of those who take flight.[36] In the

[FIGS 15, 16]

cartoon it is possible to discern rage, disdain and vindictiveness in the men no less than in the horses, two of which are entangled by their forelegs, using their teeth to fight no less intensely* than

* showing no
less vengeance

the riders who contest the standard. The staff of the standard has been gripped by the hand of a soldier, who with the power of his shoulders, while putting his horse to flight, has twisted his body to seize the staff to wrench it forcefully from the hands of four men, of whom two defend it, each grasping it with one hand while with the other they raise their swords in the air, intending to sever the staff. At the same time, an old soldier with a red beret, crying out, holds the staff with one hand and with the other lifts a cutlass to strike a savage blow to sever completely the two hands of those of the men who forcefully gnash their teeth while striving with ferocious gestures to defend their standard.[37] In addition, on the ground among the legs of the horses there are two foreshortened figures who fight each other, in such a way that the man on the ground has the other on top of him. The latter raises his arm as high as he can to stab his dagger with the greatest force into the other's throat to terminate his life. This other man, thrashing with his arms and legs, does what he can to avoid being killed.

It is impossible to convey adequately the draftsmanship with which Leonardo designed the costumes of the soldiers, diversely varied by him, similarly the crests of the helmets and other ornaments, to say nothing of the incredible mastery he showed in the form and lineaments of horses. Leonardo, better than any other master, showed the boldness, muscularity and gentle beauty of horses. He drew their anatomy by flaying them, alongside the anatomy of humans, and laid bare both one and the other in true modern light. It is said that to design the cartoon he made a most ingenious structure, which rose when drawn together and lowered itself when widened.[38] Deciding that he would prefer to paint with oil on the wall, he compounded a gross mixture to bind the colours to the wall. As he continued to paint and began to apply pigments in this way, he had to abandon his work in a short time, seeing that it was falling into ruin.

[FIG. 38]

Leonardo exhibited great courage in all his deeds and was most generous. It is said that when he went to the bank for his salary, which he received every month from Piero Soderini, the cashier gave him some paper rolls of small change, which he did not wish to accept, saying that 'I am no penny painter'. When he was accused of cheating Soderini, and there was murmuring against him, Leonardo arranged that he and his friends should collect the money and take it back to recompense Soderini. Piero did not wish to accept it.

He went to Rome with Duke Giuliano de' Medici on the election of Pope Leo [X], who was occupied with philosophical pursuits, above all alchemy. There Leonardo invented a wax paste, and while he wandered around he fashioned thin-skinned animals that were then fully inflated with wind, which he let fly in the air, but when the wind was exhausted they fell to the ground. Taking a very bizarre green lizard, which was found

38

*Studies of Expression and Motion: Heads of Horses, a Lion and Man
and Rearing Horses, and Plan of a Building, c.* 1503–4. Pen and
ink with wash and red chalk, 19.6 × 30.8 cm (7¾ × 12⅛ in.).

by a vineyard worker in the Belvedere, he made wings that he attached to its back using scales scraped from other lizards and a mixture of quicksilver. The wings quivered as it moved and wandered about. Having made eyes, horns and beard, he tamed it and kept it in a box, and all the friends to whom he showed it flew from it in fear. He often used to purge the fat meticulously from the guts of a bullock and he made them so thin that they could be squeezed in the palm of one's hand. And having secreted a pair of smith's bellows in another room, attached to one end of the guts, he inflated them to fill a room that was enormous, so that anyone who was there had to retreat into a corner. Such transparent and inflated objects – which occupied only a little space at the beginning but then came to occupy a great space – he likened to virtue. He made an infinite number of these crazy things, and he occupied himself with mirrors, and he explored strange ways of finding oils for painting and varnishes to preserve the finished works.

At this time for Messer Baldassarre Turini from Pescia, who was a papal officer for [Pope] Leo, he made a small picture of Our Lady with her Son in her arms with infinite diligence and skill.[39] But, whether we should blame the person who applied the gesso [to the panel] or Leonardo's capricious mixing of primers and pigment, it is today very deteriorated. And in another small picture he portrayed a little boy, which is beautiful and marvellously graceful.[40] These two pictures are both in Pescia with Messer Giulio Turini.

It is said that, having received a commission for a work from the Pope,* he immediately began to distil oil and herbs to make

* It is said that he received a commission for a work from the Pope, for which

the varnish, which is why Pope Leo said, 'Alas, this man will not do anything, in that he begins by thinking about the end before beginning the work'. There was a great disdain between Michelangelo Buonarroti and Leonardo, and on account of the competition Michelangelo left Florence, having been given leave by Giuliano to discuss the façade of San Lorenzo with the Pope.

Leonardo then decided to leave, and went to France, where the king possessed some of his works, and was very affectionate towards him. The king wanted him to paint the cartoon of St Anne, but, as was customary, he spent a long time only talking about it.[41] Finally, having become old, he fell ill for many

[FIG. 14]   months, and seeing himself close to death, debating matters of the Church and returning to the righteous path, there was nothing else but to turn, with much sobbing, to the Christian faith, wherefore he wished to be fully cognisant of all things Catholic, the road to goodness and the holy Christian religion, and with many laments he confessed and expressed contrition. Even if he could not sustain himself on his feet and had to be supported by friends and servants, he resolved to take the Holy Sacrament outside his bed. The king, who had often lovingly visited him, arrived one day and out of reverence for the king Leonardo raised himself in bed to a sitting position, speaking of his illness and the symptoms he was exhibiting, and above all how he had given offense to God and to the people of the world for not having worked on his art as he should have done. Then he was overcome by a paroxysm, the herald of death. At this the king arose and held his head to comfort him, granting him special favour and

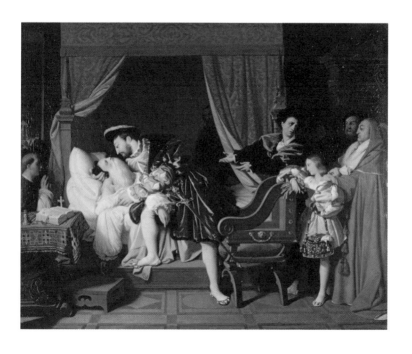

39
Jean-Auguste-Dominique Ingres, *The Death of Leonardo da Vinci*, 1818.
Oil on canvas, 40 × 50.5 cm (15¾ × 19⅞ in.).

lightening his suffering. Leonardo's spirit, divine as it was and understanding that he could not receive greater honour, expired at the age of seventy-five in the arms of the king.[42]

The loss of Leonardo saddened beyond measure all those who had known him, because there never was anyone who had brought such honour to painting. With the radiance of his aura, such was his great beauty, he lifted every sad soul, and with his words he could persuade any obdurate mind to say either yes or no. With his powers, he could quell any violent rage. With his right hand he could bend the iron ring of a door-bell set in a wall, and a horseshoe as if it were lead. With his liberality, he sheltered and nourished every friend, poor or rich, providing they had individual merit and worth. With every action he adorned and gave honour to every mean and bare habitation. Truly Florence received its greatest gift with the birth of Leonardo, and lost infinitely more with his death.

In the art of painting, he contributed a certain shadowed manner of colouring in oil, by which he gave a special power and relief to modern figure-painting. In statuary, he proved himself in the three figures in bronze which are over the north door of San Giovanni [the Baptistery], made by Giovan Francesco Rustici but shaped with Leonardo's advice, which were the most beautiful casts in design and finish that contemporaries had seen. From Leonardo we have knowledge of the anatomies of horses and men in a more complete way. Overall, his attributes were so divine – even though he performed more with words than with the things that he made – that his fame will never be extinguished. For this reason Messer Giambattista Strozzi wrote as below:*

[FIG. 39]

[FIG. 17]

* it was said on one of his epitaphs:

This man alone vanquished
All the others; he vanquished Phidias, vanquished Apelles,
And all their victorious flock.[43]

And yet another one, truly honouring him, read:

Leonardo da Vinci. What else?
Divine genius, divine hand, he was worthy of dying in
the royal bosom.
Virtue and fortune ensured that he obtained this tomb
at the greatest expense.
You know his nation and his country; and vast glory
is known even to you. For Leonardo is covered by this
ground. You can perceive the shadows in his paintings
and his learned hand applied its colours in oil, superior
to others. He knew how to imprint the bodies of men and
gods onto bronze and to infuse life into pictured horses.[44]

LEONARDO'S LIFE
KEY DATES AND WORKS

Works of art in **bold italics** were known or seemingly known to Vasari.

Works of art in *italics* are not mentioned by Vasari.

Known works are followed by their current location in brackets.

1452
On Saturday 15 April, around 10.30 p.m., Leonardo is born in Vinci out of wedlock. Leonardo's father is Ser Piero di Antonio da Vinci (1427–1504), a notary working in Florence, and his mother is a young orphan, Caterina. The baby is publicly baptized on the Sunday, with six prominent godparents.

1457
On 28 February, Leonardo is listed in Vinci as a dependent in the tax assessment of his grandfather, Antonio.

First Florentine Period
(c. 1464/69–81/83)

c. 1469
Leonardo moves to Florence at an unknown date and enters the workshop of Andrea del Verrocchio. At some point in the next four years he contributes substantially to Verrocchio's painting of *The Baptism of Christ* (Florence, Uffizi).

1472
Leonardo appears in the account book of the painters' confraternity, the Compagnia di San Luca, in Florence.

1473
On 5 August, Leonardo inscribes a mountainous landscape drawing: 'day of Saint Mary of the Snows / day of 5 August 1473' (Uffizi). He paints *The Madonna and Child with the Vase of Flowers* (Munich, Alte Pinakothek).

1476
On 9 April and 7 June, Leonardo is among those charged with homosexual activity with a seventeen-year-old apprentice in a goldsmith's workshop. The charge is not followed up.

Leonardo remains in Verrocchio's workshop. Around this time he paints the *Annunciation* (Uffizi).

1478
In January, Leonardo earns a commission for an altarpiece in the Chapel of San Bernardo in the Palazzo della Signoria of Florence. Leonardo receives a payment on 16 March, but there is no other evidence of work on the commission.

A drawing in the Uffizi is inscribed: '…ber 1478, I began the two Virgin Marys'. One of them may be the *Benois Madonna* (St Petersburg, Hermitage).

Around this time the *Portrait of Ginevra de' Benci* was painted.

1481

In July, Leonardo signs an interim agreement about the *Adoration of the Magi* for the main altar of San Donato in Scopeto, on the outskirts of Florence. Between June and September, payments in money and commodities (including wine) are made for work on the altarpiece.

Before and around this time, he begins to explore aspects of technology (civil and military) and science, including anatomy.

The unfinished *St Jerome* (Rome, Vatican) may date from this time.

First Milanese Period (1481/83–99)

1481/83

Between September 1481 and April 1483, Leonardo leaves Florence for Milan.

1483

On 25 April, with the brothers Evangelista and Giovanni Ambrogio de Predis, Leonardo signs the contract to decorate a large altarpiece for the Confraternity of the Immaculate Conception in their chapel in San Francesco Grande in Milan. The central painting is to portray the Madonna and Child. The painting he begins is the *Virgin of the Rocks* (Paris, Louvre), which may be the 'Nativity' sent by Ludovico Sforza as a wedding present to Emperor Maximilian I.

1483–90

At some point Leonardo enters the court of Ludovico Sforza, *de facto* ruler of Milan. He writes to Ludovico claiming mastery of a wide range of military engineering. His range of intellectual and practical pursuits widens and deepens, not least in the field of anatomy. A series of skull studies are dated 1489, and we have the first of his surviving series of notebooks, which deals with a diverse range of artistic, technological and scientific subjects, including the flying machine.

He paints the *Portrait of a Musician* (Milan, Biblioteca Ambrosiana), *c.* 1483.

1487

Leonardo prepares designs and a wooden model for the domed crossing tower (*tiburio*) of Milan Cathedral. Payments are recorded on 30 July, 8 August, 18 August, 27 August, 28 September, 30 September, January 1488 and May 1490. He does not receive the commission.

1489

On 22 July, the Florentine ambassador to the Sforza court in Milan writes to Lorenzo de' Medici in Florence stating that the Duke has entrusted Leonardo with the model of the *equestrian memorial* to his father, but still needs 'a master or two capable of doing such work'.

1490

On 22 July, Salaì (Gian Giacomo Caprotti da Oreno), ten years old, arrives in Leonardo's workshop as a trainee. On 7 September, Salaì steals a silverpoint drawing stylus from one of Leonardo's assistants, and on 2 April 1491 he steals another from a different assistant.

Around this time, Leonardo paints the portrait of the duke's mistress, *Cecilia Gallerani* (Lady with the Ermine, Cracow, Czartoryski Museum).

1491

Leonardo designs a festival and tournament for the wedding of Ludovico Sforza and Beatrice d'Este on 26 January.

In an undated letter, Leonardo and Giovanni Ambrogio de Predis complain to Ludovico Sforza about the Confraternity of the Immaculate Conception's low valuation for the *Virgin of the Rocks* and two paintings of angels.

1493

In November, Leonardo's full-scale *model of the Sforza Horse* is displayed under a triumphal arch inside Milan Cathedral for the marriage of Ludovico's niece, Bianca Maria Sforza, to the Emperor Maximilian I.

On 20 December, Leonardo decides to cast the *Sforza Horse* on its side and without the tail.

1494

On 17 November, Ludovico Sforza sends the bronze for the *Sforza Horse* to his father-in-law, Ercole I d'Este, Duke of Ferrara, to make cannons.

1495

Leonardo probably goes to Florence, as a consultant for the building of the Sala del Gran Consiglio for the new Florentine Republic.

Giovanni Donato da Montorfano signs and dates the *Crucifixion* fresco on the south wall of the Refectory of Santa Maria delle Grazie (opposite the wall on which Leonardo would paint his *Last Supper*). The *Portraits of Ludovico Sforza, Beatrice d'Este and their Two Sons* are later inserted in the foreground, probably by Leonardo's studio, but are now badly deteriorated.

1496

On 8 and 14 June, Leonardo is decorating rooms in the Castello Sforzesco, but it is suggested that Perugino might be approached instead.

Around this time, Leonardo portrays *Bianca Sforza* ('*La Bella Principessa*') in ink and chalks on vellum (private collection). The illegitimate daughter of Ludovico, she marries Galeazzo da Sanseverino but dies just a few months after the wedding.

1497

On 29 June, the Duke expresses his hope that Leonardo will soon finish the *Last Supper*.

1498

On 8 February, Fra Luca Pacioli dedicates to Ludovico his *De Divina Proportione*, with illustrations of the regular geometrical solids by Leonardo. Pacioli estimates that the *Sforza Horse* (without its rider) is to be over 7 m (23 ft) high.

On 22 March, a letter addressed to the Duke states that Leonardo's work on the *Last Supper* in the Refectory of Santa Maria delle Grazie should be brought to completion.

On 20, 21 and 23 April, Leonardo is at work on the murals in the *Saletta Negra* ('little back room') and the *Sala delle Asse* ('room of the boards', painted with a bower of trees with entwined branches and heraldic motifs in the northwest tower of the Castello Sforzesco).

On 26 and 29 April, Isabella d'Este, Marchioness of Mantua, asks Cecilia Gallerani to send Leonardo's portrait so that she might compare it with ones by Bellini.

The portrait now known as *La Belle Ferronière* (Paris, Louvre), identifiable as Lucrezia Crivelli, the Duke's mistress, was painted around this time.

1499

On 26 April, Ludovico Sforza has given Leonardo a vineyard on the outskirts of Milan.

On 9 and 10 September, the French troops of Louis XII storm the city, led by the Milanese mercenary general Gian Giacomo Trivulzio, for whom Leonardo was later to plan an equestrian monument.

In October, Louis XII enters Milan. Leonardo sends money to his account at the Hospital of Santa Maria Nuova in Florence. He leaves Milan with Fra Luca Pacioli.

Second Florentine Period (1500–1506/7)

1500

In February, Leonardo stays in Mantua as the guest of Marchioness Isabella d'Este.

On 13 March, Isabella d'Este receives a letter from Venice stating that Leonardo had with him his *Portrait Drawing of Isabella*.

Leonardo works for the Venetian Republic on defences against the Turks in the Friuli region, where he witnesses a competition for mills that run by perpetual motion.

On 24 April, Leonardo arrives in Florence, and probably resides in Santissima Annunziata, where he draws and exhibits a cartoon of the *Virgin and Child with St Anne*.

1501

On 28 March, Isabella d'Este asks Fra Pietro da Novellara (Head of the Carmelites in Florence) about Leonardo's activities. On 3 April,

Fra Pietro replies that Leonardo is at work on a (lost) cartoon for a *Virgin and Child with St Anne and a Lamb*.

On 14 April Fra Pietro tells Isabella that Leonardo is working on the *Madonna of the Yarnwinder* for Florimond Robertet, secretary to King Louis XII. (The Madonna is known in two largely autograph versions in private collections.) Fra Pietro also reports that Leonardo is much involved with mathematics.

1502

Between May and 18 August, Cesare Borgia, Captain of the Papal Armies, names Leonardo as architect and engineer in the Marche and Romagna. From July to September, Leonardo travels to Urbino, Cesena, Porto Cesenatico, Pesaro and Rimini for Cesare.

1503

In February, Leonardo returns to Florence.

On 9 March and 23 June, the notary for the Confraternity of the Immaculate Conception in Milan summarizes the legal situation in the dispute over the *Virgin of the Rocks*.

On 24 July, Leonardo and others demonstrate competing schemes for the *canalization of the Arno*. During July he is paid by the Signoria of Florence for his work on diverting the Arno near Pisa, and is reinscribed in the account book of the painters' confraternity.

In October, Agostino Vespucci records that Leonardo has begun the portrait of Francesco del Giocondo's wife, **Mona Lisa**, and a *St Anne*, and has been commissioned to paint the *Battle of Anghiari* in the Sala del Gran Consiglio.

On 24 October, he receives keys to the large Sala del Papa and other rooms in Santa Maria Novella, Florence, which will serve as his workshop and residence while working on his cartoon for the *Battle of Anghiari*.

At some point during this period he begins to paint *Leda and the Swan*, probably not finished until after 1513 (now lost).

1504

On 25 January, Leonardo attends a meeting to determine the placement of Michelangelo's *David*.

Between February and October, Leonardo receives a salary for work on the cartoon for the *Battle of Anghiari*. On 28 February he receives payments for his ingenious scaffolding from which he could draft the huge cartoon, and for a very large quantity of paper.

On 4 May, the Signori of the Florentine Republic, led by Niccolò Machiavelli, produce an interim agreement that summarizes the state of Leonardo's work on the *Battle of Anghiari* and what he was to do.

On 30 June, 30 August and 30 December, further payments are recorded for Leonardo's work on the *Battle of Anghiari*.

Interrupting his work, he goes
to Piombino as a military engineer
at the request of Jacopo IV Appiani,
Lord of Piombino and ally of Florence.

In the evening of 9 July, Leonardo
records that his father, Ser Piero di
Antonio da Vinci, has died in Florence.

In August, Leonardo's uncle,
Francesco, bequeaths him property,
which initiates a long-running
legal dispute with his half-brothers.

On 30 November, Leonardo records
that he believes he has solved the
problem of squaring the circle. This
proves not to be the case.

1505

On 28 February, 14 March and 30 April
Leonardo is involved in the painting
of the *Battle of Anghiari* in the council
hall. Expenses for Leonardo's scaffolding
and painting are reimbursed, with
names of his assistants, Raffaello
d'Antonio di Biagio, Ferrando Spagnolo
and Tommaso di Giovanni, who 'grinds
colours' for Ferrando.

On 6 June, Leonardo records that
when he started to paint in the hall on
that particular day the weather became
extremely severe. During the torrential
storm, the cartoon is torn.

On 31 August and 31 October, more
payments are made for Leonardo's
work on the painting of the *Battle
of Anghiari*.

At some point in 1505 or 1506,
Leonardo ceases painting the *Battle
of Anghiari*. Around this time, or
somewhat earlier, he begins the *Salvator
Mundi* (Louvre Abu Dhabi).

Second Milanese Period
(1506/7–13)

1506

On 13 February, Leonardo designates
Giovanni Ambrogio de Predis to
represent him in the dispute with
the Confraternity of the Immaculate
Conception in Milan, and arbitrators
are appointed.

On 27 April, de Predis comes to
an agreement with the Confraternity
regarding the *Virgin of the Rocks*,
which is still unfinished. An agreement
between Leonardo and the Signoria of
Florence indicates that Leonardo can
visit Milan for three months.

On 18 August, Charles II d'Amboise,
French governor of Milan, writes
to the Signoria in Florence requesting
Leonardo's services. On 19 and
28 August, the French arrange for the
Signoria to permit Leonardo to go to
Milan. Leonardo sets out for Milan
in early September. Charles d'Amboise
commissions Leonardo to design
a suburban villa and garden.

On 9 October, Piero Soderini,
Gonfaloniere of Florence, accuses
Leonardo of breaking his promises.

On 16 December, in a letter
to the Signoria, Charles d'Amboise
expresses his satisfaction with
Leonardo's work.

1507

On 12, 14 and 22 January, in letters
involving the Florentine Ambassador
to France, the Signoria of Florence
and the French court, it is agreed that

Leonardo should stay in Milan to serve the French.

In March, Leonardo returns with Salaì to Florence.

On 23 July, Leonardo seems to be back in Milan.

On 26 July, Florimond Robertet requests on behalf of the king that 'our dear and well-loved Leonardo da Vinci, painter and engineer of our trust' should serve the king in Milan.

On 3 August, an arbitrator is appointed in a dispute between Leonardo and Giovanni Ambrogio de Predis about the *Virgin of the Rocks*.

Leonardo produces stage designs for *Orpheus*, a play by Angelo Poliziano, with a set for a 'mountain that opens'.

On 15 August, Charles II d'Amboise demands that the Signoria permit Leonardo to return to Milan 'because he is obliged to make a painting' for the king.

On 26 August the arbitration decisions regarding the *Virgin of the Rocks* are summarized.

Around this time, Leonardo meets the young nobleman Francesco Melzi, who was to become his devoted pupil, companion, and major heir.

Leonardo returns to Florence at some point in the winter of 1507/8, and dissects an old man who claimed to be 100 years old (the 'centenarian') at the Hospital of Santa Maria Nuova.

Among other scientific work, Leonardo undertakes studies of the complex optics of the eye.

1508

On 22 March, Leonardo is staying at the house of Piero di Braccio Martelli in Florence and contributes to Giovan Francesco Rustici's three bronze figures of the *Preaching of St John the Baptist* for the Baptistery in Florence.

On 23 April, Leonardo is known to have returned to Milan to serve Louis XII. Probably around this time he resumes work on the project for a *Virgin, Child and St Anne*. The version now in the Louvre was probably not finished until much later.

From July until April 1509, he records his salary from the French king.

On 18 August, de Predis and Leonardo receive permission to remove the second version of the *Virgin of the Rocks* newly installed in San Francesco Il Grande, so that de Predis can copy it under Leonardo's supervision. The version of the painting that finally occupies its place in the confraternity's altarpiece is the one now in the National Gallery, London.

On 12 October, Leonardo authorizes the final settlement for the *Virgin of the Rocks*, and on 23 October de Predis receives a final payment for his copy.

1510

Leonardo continues to work on technological and scientific projects, including anatomy, geology and geometry. He records that he intends 'in this winter' to bring his anatomical work to a conclusion, and has been collaborating with the anatomist Marcantonio della Torre.

He is granted an annual salary by the French state.

1511

On 10 and 18 December, Leonardo records that invading Swiss soldiers have started fires in the city of Milan, ending the French domination of Milan.

Leonardo and his household reside for a time at the Melzi family villa in Vaprio d'Adda, outside Milan, where he plans a canal to bypass a rocky section of the river.

Roman Period (1513–16)

1513

On 24 September, Leonardo records that 'I departed from Milan to go to Rome' accompanied by Melzi, Salaì and two other members of his household, probably passing through Florence on the way.

On 1 December, Leonardo is in Rome in the service of Giuliano de' Medici (brother of Pope Leo X), with a workshop in the Belvedere of the Vatican Palace.

In this year he undertook some of his major studies of the heart, its valves and the motions of the blood.

1514

Resident in Rome, Leonardo also travels in the service of Giuliano in connection with military and civil engineering, including the draining of the Pontine Marshes near Rome.

He works on *burning mirrors* for Giuliano, which occasions a dispute with a German mirror-maker.

1515

On 9 January, Leonardo notes that Giuliano de' Medici departed at dawn from Rome in order to marry in Savoy.

On 12 July, a *mechanical lion* by Leonardo is presented as a gift from Lorenzo di Piero de' Medici for the entry of King Francis I into Lyons on his return from Italy.

On 30 November, Pope Leo X makes a triumphal entry into Florence. Leonardo and Giuliano de' Medici are among the papal entourage.

Leonardo plans a new palace for Lorenzo di Piero de' Medici, opposite Michelozzo's Palazzo Medici.

Between 7 and 17 December, Leonardo may have travelled to Bologna, where the Pope is to meet the French King.

1516

Leonardo records the solution to a mathematical problem: the equivalence of rectilinear and curvilinear areas.

On 17 March, Giuliano de' Medici dies, and Leonardo writes that 'the Medici made me, and destroyed me'.

French Period (1516–19)

1516

Leonardo goes to France as '*paintre du Roy*' for King Francis I. He is accompanied by Melzi and Salaì.

1517

On Ascension Day in May, Leonardo records that he is in Amboise and Cloux (Clos Lucé), where he lives in the manor house.

On 1 October, a letter describes a celebration for King Francis I in Argentan, at which Leonardo's mechanical lion walked forward to open its breast, 'and in the inside it was all blue, which signified love'.

On 10 October, Leonardo, as an ornament of the court, receives a visit from the touring party of Cardinal Luigi d'Aragona. One of the secretaries, Antonio de Beatis, records the event in his diary. They were shown three paintings, a portrait of 'a *certain Florentine woman* done from life at the request of the said magnificent Giuliano de' Medici', a young *St John the Baptist*, and a *Virgin, Child and St Anne*. They were also shown manuscripts, most notably those that dealt with anatomy. Because of a paralysis on his right side, 'he can no longer paint with the sweetness of style that he used to have, and he can only make drawings and teach others'.

On 29 December, de Beatis visits Leonardo's *Last Supper* in Milan, noting that 'although most excellent, it is beginning to deteriorate'.

During his time in France, Leonardo spends time in Romorantin for the project to build a great palace for Francis I, which would involve substantial hydraulic engineering.

For the years 1517–18, he is in receipt of a very substantial stipend from the king, with Melzi and Salaì also receiving good salaries.

1518

On 17 January, in celebration of the wedding of Lorenzo de' Medici and Maddalena de la Tour d'Auvergne, niece of King Francis I, Leonardo devises a visual show at Clos Lucé with a representation of the heavens.

On 24 June, Leonardo writes that he has left Romorantin to go to the manor house of Cloux at Amboise.

1519

On 23 April, sixty-seven years old and ill, Leonardo draws up his will, which includes provision for the saying of masses. Melzi is the beneficiary of Leonardo's written and drawn legacy.

On 2 May, Leonardo dies in Clos Lucé and is buried in the cloister of the church Saint-Florentin at Amboise (now destroyed).

On 1 June, Francesco Melzi writes movingly to Leonardo's half-brother, Ser Giuliano da Vinci, to notify the family of Leonardo's death.

NOTES

Introduction

1 *Le vite de' più eccellenti architettori, pittori, et scultori Italiani, da Cimabue insino a' tempi nostri, descritti in lingua Toscana, da Giorgio Vasari pittore aretino. Con la sua utile & necessario introduzioni a le arti loro.*

2 Giovio's writings on artists were not published until 1781. See P. Giovio, *Scritti d'arte*, ed. S. Maffei, Pisa, p. 234; trans. T. Frangenberg in *The Lives of Leonardo*, p. 4.

3 K. Frey, *Der Literarische Nachlass Giorgio Vasaris*, Munich, 1923, I, p. 197, XCIII.

4 Frescoes commissioned by Cardinal Alessandro Farnese for the large reception room in the Palazzo della Cancelleria, glorifying his grandfather, Pope Paul III.

5 C. Hope, 'The Biography of Leonardo in Vasari's *Vite*', in *The Lives of Leonardo*, pp. 11–28, with further references to Hope's studies of the authorship of the *Lives*.

6 See T. Frangenberg, 'Bartolo, Giambullari and the Prefaces to Vasari's Lives', *Journal of the Warburg and Courtauld Institutes*, 56, 2002, pp. 244–58.

7 See the research tools on the Vasari site of the Scuola Normale Superiore, Pisa: http://vasari.sns.it/consultazione/Vasari/ricerca.html.

8 For this and other key terms, see M. Kemp, 'From Mimesis to Fantasia; the Quattrocento Vocabulary of Invention, Imagination and Creation in the Visual Arts', *Viator* VIII, 1977, pp. 347–98.

9 L. Ghiberti, *I Commentarii, Biblioteca Nazionale Centrale di Firenze, II, I, 333*, ed. Lorenzo Bartoli, Florence, 1998.

10 A. Manetti, *The Life of Brunelleschi*, ed. H. Saalman, trans. C. Engass, University Park and London, 1970.

11 F. Albertini, *Memoriale di molte statue e pitture della Città di Firenze*, ed. L. Mussini and L. Piaggio, Florence, 1863.

12 Most notably the '*Libro di Antonio Billi*', which contains short accounts of Florentine artists in chronological succession (ed. C. Frey, Berlin, 1892); and the amplified accounts in the Anonimo Gaddiano, now thought to be Bernardo Vecchietti (C. Fabriczy, *Il Codice Anonimo Gaddiano XVII, 17 nella Bibliotheca Nazionale di Firenze*, Florence, 1893). See Hope in *The Lives of Leonardo*, pp. 11–12, for Vasari's sources, also positing a lost text. For a wide-ranging discussion of Vasari's sources, see Rubin chapter III.

13 R. Scorza, 'Vincenzo Borghini's Collection of Paintings, Drawings and Wax models: New Evidence from Manuscript Sources', *Journal of the Warburg and Courtauld Institutes*, LXVI, 2003, pp. 63–122.

14 Borghini in Rubin, p. 192.

15 See M. Ruffini, *Art Without an Author: Vasari's Lives and Michelangelo's Death*, New York, 2011.

16   For a detailed analysis of the input of Bartoli and Giambullari, see T. Frangenberg, 'Bartolo, Giambullari and the Prefaces to Vasari's Lives', *Journal of the Warburg and Courtauld Institutes*, 56, 2002, pp. 244–58.

17   B. Varchi, *Due lezzioni di M Benedetto Varchi...*, Florence, 1549.

18   '*Di Nuovo...Rivise Et Ampliate Con i Ritratti loro Et con l'aggiunta delle Vite de'vivi, & de'morti Dall'anno 1550 insino 1567...Con le tavole in ciascun volume, Delle cose più Notabili, De' Ritratti, Delle vite degli Artefici, a dei Luohgi dove sono l'opere loro'.* For the changes in the 1568 edition, see Rubin chapter V.

19   M. Kemp, 'Virtuous Artists and Virtuous Art', in *Notions of Decorum in Renaissance Narrative Art,* ed. F. Ames Lewis and A. Bednarek, London, 1992, pp. 15–23.

20   S. Gregory, 'The Outer Man Tends to be a Guide to the Inner: the Woodcut Portraits in Vasari's Lives as Parallel Texts', *The Rise of the Image: Essays on the History of the Illustrated Book*, ed. R. Palmer and T. Frangenberg, Aldershot, 2003: http://alonso.stfx.ca/sgregory/PDFs/Parallel%20Texts.pdf; and C. Hope, 'Historical Portraits in the "Lives" and in the Frescoes of Giorgio Vasari', in *Giorgio Vasari: tra decorazione ambientale e storiografia artistica*, Florence, 1985, pp. 321–38.

21   Florence, Archivio di Stato Notarile antecosimiano 16828, c. 43v. I am grateful to Giuseppe Pallanti for this reference.

22   L. C. Ragghianti, *Il Libro de' Disegni del Vasari*, 2 vols, Florence, 1974. See also *Giorgio Vasari. Principi, letterati e artsti nelle carte di Giorgio Vasari. Casa Vasari...* exhib. cat. Florence, 1981.

23   *Anonimo Gaddiano*, ed. Frey, p. 110.

24   Giambattista Giraldi, *Discorsi ... intorno al comporre de i romanzi, delle comedie, e delle tragedie*, Venice, 1554, pp. 194–96.

25   For Leonardo's *Treatise* in mid 16th-century Florence, see A. Sconza, 'The Earliest Abridged Copies of the *Libro de Pittura* in Florence', in *The Fabrication of Leonardo da Vinci's Trattato della pittura*, 2 vols, Leiden, 2018, I, chapter 5, esp. pp. 242–80.

26   For Vasari and his contacts at Santissima Annunziata, see M. Kemp and G. Pallanti, *Mona Lisa. The People and the Painting*, Oxford, 2017, pp. 52–54.

27   C. Vecce, *Leonardo*, Rome, 2006, pp. 331–32.

28   For the epitaphs, see Maia W. Gahtan, 'Epitaphs in Giorgio Vasari's *Lives*', *Journal of Art Historiography*, V, 2011, pp. 1–24. There were three epitaphs on Leonardo in the 1550 edition, only one of which survived.

29   In the Italian: '*un certo fondamento terribile di concetti'.*

Translation

1   Here Vasari is amplifying the standard astrological determination of character by the positions of the planets at the moment of birth ('in a natural way') with a divine creation that transcends the normal process ('supernaturally'). Vasari's introductory sentences are notably convoluted and have been untangled in the translation to a degree that makes them easier to understand without radically recasting them.

2 The direct reference is to the abacus, used for arithmetical calculations. It may also allude to Leonardo's attendance at an 'abacus school' for a basic education in numeracy and literacy.

3 The '*lira*' is the *lira da braccio*, an ancestor of the viola that was used for improvised music and song (see fig. 9).

4 His known work on the Arno canal, as in the illustrated drawing, does not belong to the early phase of his career, as is the case with much of the engineering mentioned at this point in the *Life*. Vasari is basing this account on the manuscripts he saw in Melzi's possession after the publication of the first edition.

5 The *Study of a Lily with the Plan of a Building* is pricked for transfer to a painting, e.g. a Madonna or an Annunciation (like that in the Uffizi), but does not correspond precisely to a known painting.

6 The illustrated drawing is one of the few engineering drawings that can be dated to the early Florentine phase of Leonardo's career.

7 The six knot engravings bear different versions of the motto.

8 In addition to the angel, it appears that Leonardo intervened extensively with oil paint in the foreground, landscape and figure of Christ.

9 No longer known.

10 In the 1550 edition, the duke's name is given as Francesco. It must be Ludovico, his son.

11 The buckler is no longer known. The price of 100 ducats is high, and 300 is implausible.

12 On the preparatory drawing at Windsor, related compositionally to the *Battle of Anghiari*, Leonardo wrote 'lower the horses'.

13 *Pinxit Virgilius Neptunum, pinxit Homerus, Dum maris undisoni per vada flectit equos. Mente quidem vates ilium conspexit uterque, Vincius ast oculis; jureque vincit eos.*

14 No longer known.

15 Known in a pupil's drawing at Windsor (12328) corrected by Leonardo, in a follower's painting in the Hermitage, St Petersburg, and in a lost drawing by Baccio Bandinelli. For a review of the Angel / St John images, see C. Pedretti and M. Melani, *L'Angelo / San Giovanni un dipinto senza committente*, Poggio a Caiano, 2016.

16 Pierfrancesco Giambullari was a literary colleague and collaborator of Vasari's.

17 Leonardo moved to Milan earlier, probably in 1482. Although Ludovico was to become Duke of Milan only in 1494, he was in effect the ruler of the city when Leonardo went there. It seems likely that Leonardo was sent to the duke by Lorenzo de' Medici, in the company of Atalante Migliorotti, a much admired singer, instrumentalist and instrument-maker who may be the subject of the *Portrait of a Musician* in the Biblioteca Ambrosiana in Milan.

18 The engraving by Marcantonio Raimondi of *Orpheus Charming the Animals* from *c.* 1508 may well be a satirical portrait of Leonardo playing the *lira da braccio*. See R. Duffin, 'Leonardo's Lira', *Magazine of the Cleveland Museum of Art*, May / June 2015, pp. 10–12: http://www. clevelandart.org/sites/default/files/ May-June_2015_magazine_web_0.pdf. The musician is attended not by the normal cluster of attentive animals but by a distracted dog and a bear that appears to be expressing itself chorally in an unwanted manner. Leonardo was the butt of at least one satirical poem in Milan.

19 It is conceivable that a *lira* could be made roughly in the shape of a horse's skull, but it would have been made not from silver but from wood, perhaps with silver decorations. I am grateful to Bonnie Blackburn for an informative discussion of the *lira*.

20 This may well be the *Virgin of the Rocks* in the Louvre, begun in 1483 for the Confraternity of the Immaculate Conception in Milan, which could have been commandeered by Ludovico as a gift for the wedding of Maximilian to Bianca Maria Sforza. The replacement painting was not delivered to the Confraternity until 1508.

21 The recent restoration, which has confirmed the extensive paint losses (the result, in large measure, of Leonardo's experimental technique), suggests that the head of Christ was finished. The early deterioration of the mural may have led observers to conclude that Christ was unfinished.

22 The portraits were painted (in oil?) on plaster inserted into Montorfano's 1495 fresco, and have largely flaked away. What remains suggests that they were painted by an able assistant in Leonardo's workshop.

23 The project was for a gigantic equestrian monument to Ludovico's father, Francesco Sforza, not one portraying Duke Ludovico himself.

24 '*che l'opra è ritardata dal desio*': Petrarch, *Trionfo d'Amore / Triumphus Cupidinis*, 3.13.9.

25 Leonardo's collaboration with Marcantonio occurred during his second period in Milan around 1510. Galen, the philosopher, was the greatest authority on the human body in classical antiquity. The illustrated study of a sectioned skull is from Leonardo's first surviving set of anatomical investigations in 1498, while the anatomy of the shoulder is from the period working with Marcantonio.

26 Francesco Melzi was from a Lombard aristocratic family, and joined Leonardo's household as a teenager after 1507. He became Leonardo's assistant and close companion. He was guardian of his master's legacy of drawings and manuscripts, compiling the *Treatise on Painting*.

He is elusive as a painter on his own account.

27 The painter's name was never inserted.

28 The identity of the Milanese painter is not known, but might have been Giovanni Paolo Lomazzo. Since Vasari describes the text as written in mirror script, it was not the prime version of the treatise neatly transcribed by Melzi.

29 Leonardo is documented as making two mechanical lions in honour of Francis I, the first for the entry of the king into Lyon in July 1515, and the second, which is described as walking forward by Vasari, for a festival in Argentan in October 1517.

30 Salaì, named after a little devil in Luigi Pulci's poem *Morgante,* was Gian Giacomo Caprotti da Oreno. He remained with Leonardo as an assistant and servant until his master's death.

31 The painting was to be for the double-sided high altar at the junction of the new choir and old nave in Santissima Annunziata. Pietro Perugino was eventually to supply paintings of *Christ's Deposition from the Cross* and the *Assumption of the Virgin.*

32 The surviving cartoon in London differs from that described here, since St John does not play with a lamb. The cartoon described by Vasari corresponds more closely to the painting of the *Virgin, Child, St Anne and a Lamb* in the Louvre, though it is Christ himself who plays with the lamb and St John is omitted. The variant compositions involving St Anne occupied Leonardo from 1499–*c.* 1517.

33 The portrait of Ginevra in Washington dates from *c.* 1478 in Leonardo's first Florentine period.

34 This is consistent with the portrait having been begun in 1503 and left unfinished when Leonardo left Florence in 1507. It was probably not wholly finished until 1513 or later.

35 The very large Sala del Gran Consiglio was built after the expulsion of the Medici in 1498. The republican government was in the hands of the *gonfalonieri* (standard-bearers) and committees of prominent citizens, of whom the leader was the Gonfaloniere di Giustizia, Piero Soderini. He was elected as 'Gonfaloniere for Life' in 1502.

36 Leonardo had been working on the cartoon in 1503, and began to paint in the hall in 1504 or 1505. Rubens's drawing in the Louvre is the most spirited rendering of Leonardo's battle, reworking an anonymous Italian drawing which was perhaps based on the cartoon. The unfinished painting remained visible until the mid 1560s, when Vasari redecorated the hall with his cycle of Medicean frescoes. The most accurate record of Leonardo's painted battle is the 'Tavola Doria' in the Uffizi. Michelangelo was commissioned to paint a companion scene, the *Battle of Cascina*, which progressed no further than a cartoon.

37 It seems that Vasari was confused about the narrative and precise identity of the combatants. The old man with the red beret is Niccolò Piccinino, the Milanese commander, while the two handsome horsemen on the right are Florentines who strive to seize the Milanese standard. The capture of the standard was a decisive event in the Florentine victory.

38 The scaffolding that supported the platform necessary to reach the top and sides of the vast cartoon was seemingly designed in the manner of a modern scissor lift.

39 No longer known.

40 Possibly identifiable as the *Boy with a Puzzle* in Elton Hall, now attributed to Bernardino Luini.

41 The painting in the Louvre, dating from late in Leonardo's career, reverts to a composition similar to that described by Vasari as exhibited in Santissima Annunziata in Florence (though omitting the infant St John of the cartoon). Leonardo wrote to the king in *c.* 1508 promising Madonnas of two different sizes.

42 Leonardo was born in 1452 and died in 1519. The painting by Ingres captures the spirit of Vasari's legendary account of Leonardo's death. Giovio's manuscript life of Leonardo records the correct age for Leonardo at his death.

43 '*VINCE COSTUI PUR SOLO / TUTTI ALTRI, VINCE FIDIA, VINCE APELLE, / E TTUTO IL LORE VITORIOSO STUOLO*', punning on Vinci – *vince* (he vanquished). Strozzi, a member of the leading Florentine family, was a poet/composer in academic circles in mid 15th-century Florence.

44 LEONARDVS VINCIVS. QVID PLVRA? DIVINVM INGENIVM, DIVINA MANVS, EMORI IN SINV REGIO MERVERE.VIRTVS ET FORTVNA HOC MONVMENTVM CONTINGERE GRAVISS[IMIS] IMPENSIS CVRAVERVNT. ET GENTEM ET PATRIAM NOSCIS; TIBI GLORIA ET INGENS NOTA EST: HAC TEGITVR NAM LEONARDVS HVMO. PERSPICVAS PICTVRAE VMBRAS OLEOQVE COLORES ILLIVS ANTE ALIOS DOCTA MANVS POSVIT. IMPRIMERE ILLE HOMINVM, DIVVM QVOQVE CORPORA IN AERE ET PICTIS ANIMAM FINGERE NOVIT EQVIS.

FURTHER READING

Leonardo's career and works

Clark's monograph remains a fine introduction: K. Clark, *Leonardo da Vinci*, ed. M. Kemp, Harmondsworth, 1988.

For the documentation, see E. Villata (ed.), *Leonardo da Vinci. I documenti e le testimonianze contemporanee*, Milan, 1999; and V. Arrighi, A. Bellinazzi and E. Villata (eds), *Leonardo da Vinci. La vera immagine: documenti e testimonianze sulla vita e sull'opera*, Florence, 2005.

For Leonardo's paintings, see F. Zöllner and J. Nathan, *Leonardo da Vinci*, Cologne, available in a number of editions, most recently in 2017.

For the drawings, see K. Clark, *The Drawings of Leonardo da Vinci in the Collection of Her Majesty the Queen at Windsor Castle*, 2nd edn with C. Pedretti, 3 vols, London and New York, 1968; and more generally, A. E. Popham, *The Drawings of Leonardo da Vinci*, ed. M. Kemp, London, 1994.

For Leonardo's own writings, see J. P. Richter, *The Literary Works of Leonardo da Vinci,* 2 vols, Oxford, 1970; and with Commentary by C. Pedretti, 2 vols, Oxford, 1977.

A selection of Leonardo's writings on painting appear in *Leonardo on Painting: An Anthology of Writings by Leonardo da Vinci with a Selection of Documents Relating to his Career as an Artist*, ed. M. Kemp,

trans. M. Kemp and M. Walker, New Haven and London, 2001.

For an overall view of Leonardo's art, science and technology, see M. Kemp, *Leonardo da Vinci: The Marvellous Works of Nature and Man*, Oxford, 2006.

Vasari's writings

For English translations, see pp. 55–58, this volume.

The two editions by Vasari himself are: *Le vite de' piú eccellenti architettori, pittori, et scultori Italiani, da Cimabue insino a' tempi nostri, descritti in lingua Toscana, da Giorgio Vasari pittore aretino. Con la sua utile & necessario introduzioni a le arti loro*, 2 vols, Florence, 1550; and *Le vite de' più eccellenti pittori, scultori, et architettori Scritte, & Di Nuovo...Rivise Et Ampliate...Con I ritratti loro, Et con l'aggiunta delle Vite de'vivi, & de'morti Dall'anno 1550 insino 1567...Con le tavole in ciascun volume, Delle cose più Notabili, De' Ritratti, Delle vite degli Artefici, a dei Luoghi dove sono l'opere loro* (title-page to Parts I and II), Florence, 1568.

Two online sources provide good digital access to the 1550 and 1568 texts of the *Lives*: http://vasari.sns. it/consultazione/Vasari/indice.html; http://www.memofonte.it/ricerche/ giorgio-vasari/ (also with the texts of Vasari's other writings).

Le vite de' più eccellenti pittori, scultori, et architettori, G. Milanesi (ed.), 9 vols, Florence, 1878–85.

Le opere di Giorgio Vasari, G. Milanesi and P. Barocchi (eds), 9 vols (1906), Florence, 1973.

K. Frey, *Der literarische Nachlass Giorgio Vasaris,* 2 vols, Munich, 1923/1930.

Le vite de' più eccellenti pittori, scultori e architettori, P. Della Pergola, L. Grassi and G. Previtali (eds), 6 vols, Novara, 1967.

Le vite de' più eccellenti pittori scultori ed architettori: nelle redazioni del 1550 and 1568, R. Bettarini and P. Barocchi (eds), 6 vols, Florence, 1966–87.

Studies of Vasari and his *Lives*

Important studies in English are:

T. S. R. Boase, *Giorgio Vasari: the Man and the Book,* Princeton, 1979.

P. Rubin, 'What Men Saw: Vasari's Life of Leonardo da Vinci and the Image of the Renaissance Artist', *Art History* XIII, 1990, pp. 36–46.

P. Rubin, *Giorgio Vasari: Art and History,* New Haven, 1995.

D. Cast, *The Delight of Art: Giorgio Vasari and the Traditions of Humanist Discourse,* University Park, PA, 2009.

M. Ruffini, *Art Without an Author: Vasari's Lives and Michelangelo's Death,* New York, 2011.

Valuable collections of essays or individual essays are:

Giorgio Vasari. Principi, letterati e artisti nelle carte di Giorgio Vasari. Casa Vasari... exhib. cat., Florence, 1981.

'"Equal Excellences": Lomazzo and the Explanation of Individual Style in the Visual Arts', *Renaissance Studies* (Society of Renaissance Studies Annual Lecture) I, 1987, pp. 1–26.

T. Frangenberg, 'Bartolo, Giambullari and the Prefaces to Vasari's Lives', *Journal of the Warburg and Courtauld Institutes* 56, 2002, pp. 244–58.

Reading Vasari, A. Barriault, A. Ladis, N. Land and J. Wood (eds), London, 2005.

C. Vecce, 'Le biografie antiche di Leonardo', in *Leonardo da Vinci: la vera immagine: documenti e testimonianze sulla vita e sull'opera,* V. Arrighi, A. Belinazzi, E. Villata (eds), Florence, 2005, pp. 62–71.

Essays by T. Frangenberg and C. Hope in *The Lives of Leonardo,* T. Frangenberg and R. Palmer (eds), *Warburg Institute Colloquia* 22, London–Turin 2013, pp. 1–28. See the review by C. Farago, 'The Absolute Leonardo', *Journal of Art Historiography* 13, December 2015.

The Ashgate Research Companion to Giorgio Vasari, ed. D. Cast, Aldershot, 2014: https://online.vitalsource.com/#/books/9781317043294/cfi/6/2!/4/2@0:0

Vasari as a painter

L. Corti, *Vasari. Catologo Completo dei dipinti,* Florence, 1989.

L. Cheney, *The Paintings of the Casa Vasari,* New York, 1985.

L. Cheney, *The Homes of Giorgio Vasari,* New York, 2006.

PICTURE CREDITS

Frontispiece Santa Maria delle Grazie, Milan
1 *The Life of Giorgio Vasari, 1568*
2 Look Die Bildagentur der Fotografen GmbH/Alamy
3 Credits to SGP
4 Palazzo Vecchio, Florence. Bridgeman Images
5 Heritage Image Partnership Ltd/Alamy
6, 7 Royal Library, Windsor
8 Uffizi Gallery, Florence
9 Cleveland Museum of Art
10–12 Royal Library, Windsor
13 National Gallery, London
14 Musée du Louvre, Paris. Photo RMN-Grand Palais (Musée du Louvre)/René-Gabriel Ojéda
15 Musée du Louvre, Paris
16 Uffizi Gallery, Florence
17 Museo dell'Opera del Duomo, Florence. Photo 2018, Scala, Florence
18 Royal Library, Windsor

19 Musée du Louvre, Paris. Photo RMN-Grand Palais (Musée du Louvre)/Jean-Gilles Berizzi
20 Biblioteca Reale, Turin. Photo 2018, White Images/Scala, Florence
21 Biblioteca Ambrosiana, Milan. Photo 2018, Veneranda Biblioteca Ambrosiana/DeAgostini Picture Library/Scala, Florence
22 National Gallery of Art, Washington, D.C. Rosenwald Collection
23 Private collection
24 Alte Pinakothek, Munich. Photo 2018, BPK, Bildagentur für Kunst, Kultur und Geschichte, Berlin/Scala, Florence
25 Royal Library, Windsor
26 Musée du Louvre, Paris
27 Christ Church Picture Gallery, Oxford
28 Uffizi Gallery, Florence. Photography Department, Uffizi Gallery, Florence
29 Musée du Louvre, Paris

30 Santa Maria delle Grazie, Milan
31–33 Santa Maria delle Grazie, Milan. Photo © Mauro Ranzani/Bridgeman Images
34 Royal Library, Windsor
35 Biblioteca Nacional, Madrid. Bridgeman Images
36 National Gallery, Washington, D.C. Ailsa Mellon Bruce Fund
37 Musée du Louvre, Paris
38 Royal Library, Windsor
39 Musée du Louvre, Paris. Mondadori Portfolio/Walter Mori/Bridgeman Images

INDEX